The Visit

Owner of Book -

Daniel Montgomery

Works by Friedrich Dürrenmatt
available from Grove Press

The Physicists
The Visit

FRIEDRICH DÜRRENMATT

The Visit
A Tragicomedy

Translated from the German by Joel Agee

Grove Press
New York

Originally published in Switzerland under the title *Der Besuch der alten Dame*, published by Verlag der Arche, Zürich 1956 and revised version by Diogenes Verlag AG, Zürich 1980. Joel Agee translation originally published in *Selected Writings, Volume 1: Plays,* 2006, by The University Chicago Press, Chicago.

Printed in the United States of America

ISBN: 978-0-8021-4426-3

Grove Press
an imprint of Grove Atlantic
154 West 14th Street
New York, NY 10011

Distributed by Publishers Group West

www.groveatlantic.com

20 21 22 23 24   15 14 13 12 11

PRODUCTION CREDITS

The Visit was performed for the first time as *Der Besuch der alten Dame* at Schauspielhaus Zürich in 1956. It was first performed in the United States on May 5, 1958, at the Lunt-Fontanne Theatre in New York in an adaptation by Maurice Valency. It was directed by Peter Brook, produced by the Producers Theatre, and designed by Teo Otto, with the following cast:

Lynn Fontanne	Claire Zachanassian
Alfred Lunt	Anton Schill
Marla Adams	Ottilie Schill
Frieda Altman	Frau Burgomaster
Jonathan Anderson	First Conductor
David Clarke	Helmesberger
Robert Donley	Townsman
Harrison Dowd	Vogel
Myles Eason	Pedro Cabral
Stanley Erickson	Mike
Howard Fischer	Doctor Nusslin
Vincent Gardenia	First Blind Man
William Hansen	Pastor
Alfred Hoffman	Second Blind Man
Lesley Hunt	First Grandchild
John Kane	Truck Driver

Gertrude Kinnell	Frau Block
Joseph Leberman	Station Master
James MacAaron	Athlete
Lois McKim	Second Grandchild
Kent Montroy	Townsman
Edward Moor	Reporter
Daphne Newton	Frau Schill
Clarence Nordstrom	The Painter
Eric Porter	Burgomaster
John Randolph	Police Chief Schultz
Milton Selzer	Wechsler
Keneth Thornett	Hofbauer
William Thourlby	Max
Ken Walken	Karl Schill
Peter Woodthorpe	Professor Muller
John Wyse	Boby

The play was revived at the Ethel Barrymore Theatre in New York on November 25, 1973. It was directed by Harold Prince and produced by the New Phoenix Repertory Co. with sets by Edward Burbridge. The role of Claire Zachanassian was played by Rachel Roberts and the role of Anton Schill was played by John McMartin.

The play was later revived at the Criterion Center Stage Right in New York on January 23, 1992. It was directed by Edwin Sherin and produced by the Roundabout Theatre Company with sets by Thomas Lynch. The role of Claire Zachanassian was played by Jane Alexander and the role of Anton Schill was played by Harris Yulin.

Characters

THE VISITORS

CLAIRE ZACHANASSIAN, *née Wäscher,*	**TOBY** ⎤ *Gum chewers*
multimillionairess (*Armenian Oil*)	**ROBY** ⎦
HER HUSBANDS VII–IX	**KOBY** ⎤ *Blind*
THE BUTLER	**LOBY** ⎦

THE VISITED

ILL	**FIRST MAN** ⎤
HIS WIFE	**SECOND MAN** ⎥ *Blind*
HIS DAUGHTER	**THIRD MAN** ⎥
HIS SON	**FOURTH MAN** ⎦
MAYOR	**PAINTER**
PASTOR	**FIRST WOMAN**
TEACHER	**SECOND WOMAN**
DOCTOR	**MISS LOUISE**
POLICEMAN	**OFFICER HAHNCKE**

THE EXTRAS

STATIONMASTER	**CONDUCTOR**
TRAIN SUPERVISOR	**BAILIFF**

THE NUISANCES

JOURNALIST I	**RADIO REPORTER**
JOURNALIST II	**CAMERAMAN**

PLACE: Güllen, a small town
TIME: The present

(Intermission after Act Two)

The Visit

ACT ONE

The ringing of a railway-station bell before the curtain rises. Then an inscription: Güllen—evidently the name of the small town whose buildings, run-down and dilapidated, are sketchily indicated in the background. The station building, equally run-down, with or without a barrier, depending on local customs; a ripped schedule on the wall, a rusty signal cabin, its door marked NO ENTRY. *In the center, just a hint of the wretched Station Road. On the left a little house, bare, with a tiled roof, ripped posters on the windowless wall. On the left a sign:* WOMEN; *on the right:* MEN. *Everything steeped in hot autumn sun. In front of the little house, a bench. On it, four men. A fifth man, indescribably disheveled (they all are), is painting red letters on a banner, evidently for a procession: "Welcome Clairie." The thunderous pounding noise of an express train rushing past. The* STATIONMASTER *salutes in front of the station. The men on the bench move their heads from left to right, following the movement of the train as it speeds past them.*

FIRST MAN   That's the "Gudrun," Hamburg–Naples.

SECOND MAN   The "Racing Roland," Venice–Stockholm, gets here at eleven twenty-seven.

THIRD MAN   The only pleasure we have left: watching trains go by.

FOURTH MAN   Five years ago the "Gudrun" and the "Racing Roland" stopped in Güllen. Also the "Diplomat" and the "Lorelei." Important express trains, all of them.

FIRST MAN   World-class trains.

Bell rings.

SECOND MAN   Not even the local trains stop now. Just two from Kaffigen and the one-thirteen from Kalberstadt.

THIRD MAN Ruined.

FOURTH MAN The Wagner Works kaput.

FIRST MAN Bockmann & Co. bankrupt.

SECOND MAN The Hopewell Foundry shut down.

THIRD MAN Living on welfare.

FOURTH MAN On soup kitchen handouts.

FIRST MAN Living?

SECOND MAN Vegetating.

THIRD MAN Rotting away.

FOURTH MAN The whole town.

Sound of a passing train. The Stationmaster salutes. The men follow the train with a movement of their heads from left to right.

FOURTH MAN The "Diplomat."

THIRD MAN And we used to be a cultural center.

SECOND MAN One of the foremost in the country.

FIRST MAN In Europe.

FOURTH MAN Goethe spent a night here. In the Golden Apostle.

THIRD MAN Brahms composed a quartet here.

Bell rings.

SECOND MAN Berthold Schwarz invented gunpowder here.

PAINTER And I was a brilliant student at the École des Beaux-Arts, and what am I doing now? Sign painting!

SECOND MAN It's about time the millionairess got here. They say she founded a hospital in Kalberstadt.

THIRD MAN And the day nursery in Kaffigen and a memorial church in the capital.

PAINTER She had her portrait painted by Zimt. That naturalist dabbler.

FIRST MAN She and her money. She owns Armenian Oil, Western Railways, the Northern Broadcasting Company, and the nightlife quarter of Bangkok.

Sounds of a train. CONDUCTOR enters from the left, looking as if he has just jumped off the train.

CONDUCTOR (*with a long-drawn cry*) Güllen!

FIRST MAN The local train from Kaffigen.

A passenger has gotten off, walks past the men on the bench from the left, disappears behind the door marked MEN.

SECOND MAN The bailiff.

THIRD MAN He's here to put a lien on the town hall.

FOURTH MAN Now we're ruined politically too.

STATIONMASTER (*raising his baton*) Stand clear!

Enter from town the MAYOR, *the* TEACHER, *the* PASTOR, *and* ILL, *a nearly sixty-five-year-old man; all shabbily dressed.*

MAYOR Our distinguished guest will be arriving on the one-thirteen local from Kalberstadt.

TEACHER We'll have the mixed choir singing, the Youth Club.

PASTOR And the fire bell ringing. It hasn't been pawned yet.

MAYOR   The town band playing on the marketplace, and the gymnastics club forming a pyramid in honor of the billionairess. Then a banquet at the Golden Apostle. Unfortunately we don't have the funds to illuminate the cathedral and the town hall for the evening.

BAILIFF (*coming out of the little house*)   Good morning, Mayor, a very good morning to you.

MAYOR   What are you doing here, bailiff?

BAILIFF   Your Honor knows that already. I'm faced with a colossal task. Just you try putting a lien on an entire town.

MAYOR   Except for an old typewriter, you won't find a thing in the town hall.

BAILIFF   Your Honor is forgetting the Güllen Historical Museum.

MAYOR   Sold off to America three years ago. Our treasury's empty. No one is paying taxes.

BAILIFF   That calls for an investigation. The country is flourishing, and Güllen with its Hopewell Foundry goes bankrupt.

MAYOR   We're baffled ourselves. It's an economic enigma.

FIRST MAN   Bet you the Freemasons rigged the whole thing.

SECOND MAN   It's a Jewish plot.

THIRD MAN   I think big business is behind it.

FOURTH MAN   International communism is pulling the strings.

Bell rings.

BAILIFF I always find something. Got eyes like a hawk. I'll have a look at the treasury. (*Off*.)

MAYOR Better he fleeces us now, than after the millionairess arrives.

The PAINTER has finished painting his sign.

ILL That, of course, just won't work, Your Honor, these words are too informal. "Welcome Claire Zachanassian" is what it should say.

FIRST MAN But she's Clairie.

SECOND MAN Clairie Wäscher.

THIRD MAN Born and bred here.

FOURTH MAN Her father was a building contractor.

PAINTER So I'll just write "Welcome Claire Zachanassian" on the back. Then, once the billionairess is touched, we can still show her the front.

SECOND MAN It's the Stockmarketeer, Zürich-Hamburg.

A new express train passes from right to left.

THIRD MAN Always on time, you can set your watch by it.

FOURTH MAN Oh please, who still wears a watch in this place?

MAYOR Gentlemen, the billionairess is our only hope.

PASTOR Except for God.

MAYOR Except for God.

TEACHER But he won't pay.

PAINTER He has forgotten us.

Fourth Man spits.

MAYOR   You used to be friendly with her, Ill, so everything depends on you.

PASTOR   But then their ways parted. I heard some vague story—do you have a confession to make to your pastor?

ILL   We were the best of friends—young and impetuous— after all, gentlemen, I was a young fellow forty-five years ago—and she, Clara, I can still see her shining through the dark on her way to meet me in Petersen's barn or walking barefoot on moss and leaves through the woods of Konradsweil with her red hair streaming behind her, slender, supple, delicate, what a ravishing little witch. It was life that separated us, nothing but life. That's how it goes.

MAYOR   I should have some details about Mrs. Zachanassian for my little speech at the banquet in the Golden Apostle. (*Takes a small notebook from his pocket.*)

TEACHER   I went through the old school records. Clara Wäscher's grades were, most unfortunately, very poor. So was her conduct. Her only passing grade was in botany and zoology.

MAYOR (*taking notes*)   Good. Passed in botany and zoology. That's good.

ILL   I can help you here, Your Honor. Clara loved justice. No doubt about it. One day they were arresting a bum. She threw rocks at the police.

MAYOR   Love of justice. Not bad. Always make an impression. But we'd better drop that bit about the police.

ILL   She was charitable too. Whatever she had, she shared. She stole potatoes for a poor widow.

6

MAYOR   A charitable disposition. This, gentlemen, I must definitely include. It's the main issue. Does anyone remember anything her father built? That would be worth mentioning.

PAINTER   Nobody.

FIRST MAN   They say he was a drunk.

SECOND MAN   His wife left him.

THIRD MAN   Died in a madhouse.

Fourth Man spits.

MAYOR (*closing his notebook*)   For my part, I'm ready—the rest is up to Ill.

ILL   I know. Get Zachanassian to cough up her millions.

MAYOR   Millions—you've got the right idea. Exactly.

TEACHER   A nursery school just isn't enough.

MAYOR   My dear Ill, you've been the most popular personality in Güllen for a long time. I will be retiring in the spring. I made contact with the opposition. We've agreed to nominate you as my successor.

ILL   But Your Honor.

TEACHER   I can only confirm this.

ILL   Gentlemen, back to business. I will first talk to Claire about our miserable situation.

PASTOR   But carefully—sensitively.

ILL   We have to be smart about this, strike the right psychological note. If we botch the welcome at the station, that alone could jinx the whole thing. The town band and the mixed choir just isn't enough.

MAYOR   Ill is right. This is an important moment, after all. Mrs. Zachanassian sets foot on her native soil, she's found her way home, is moved, tears in her eyes, she sees the old familiar sights. I, of course, won't be standing here in my shirtsleeves like this, I'll be wearing a formal black suit with a top hat, my wife beside me, my two grandchildren in front of me, all in white, with roses. My God, I hope it all falls into place at the right time.

Bell rings.

FIRST MAN   The "Racing Roland."

SECOND MAN   Venice-Stockholm eleven twenty-seven.

PASTOR   Eleven twenty-seven! We still have nearly two hours to put on our Sunday best.

MAYOR   Kühn hoists the "Welcome Claire Zachanassian" banner, together with Hauser. (*Points at the fourth man.*)   The others should preferably wave their hats. But please, no shouting like last year for the Government Commission, the impact amounted to zero, and to this day we have not received a subsidy. Excessive high spirits are out of place here; the occasion calls for an inward joy, close to sobbing, heartfelt sympathy with this child of our town who has returned to us. Be natural, be sincere, but don't slip up on the timing; make sure the fire bell goes off right after the mixed choir. And above all . . .

The thunder of the oncoming train drowns out his speech. Screeching brakes. Dumbfounded astonishment on all faces. The five men leap up from the bench.

PAINTER   The Express!

8

FIRST MAN   Stopping!

SECOND MAN   In Güllen!

THIRD MAN   The most poverty-stricken—

FOURTH MAN   —lousiest—

FIRST MAN   —pathetic dump on the Venice-Stockholm route!

STATIONMASTER   The laws of nature have been suspended. The "Racing Roland" is supposed to show up as it comes around the bend at Leuthenau, zoom past here, and vanish again as a dark dot in Pückenried Valley.

Enter, right, CLAIRE ZACHANASSIAN, sixty-two, red-haired, pearl necklace, huge gold bracelets, extravagantly made up, quite impossible but just for that reason a grande dame, with a peculiar grace, despite her grotesque appearance. Followed by her entourage, THE BUTLER, Boby, about eighty years old, with black glasses, her HUSBAND VII (tall, slim, black moustache) with a complete set of fishing tackle. An agitated TRAIN SUPERVISOR with a red cap and a red pouch accompanies the group.

CLAIRE ZACHANASSIAN   Am I in Güllen?

TRAIN SUPERVISOR   Madam, you pulled the emergency brake.

CLAIRE ZACHANASSIAN   I always pull the emergency brake.

TRAIN SUPERVISOR   I protest. Vigorously. In this country, you don't pull the emergency brake, not even in an emergency. Staying on schedule is our first principle. May I request an explanation?

CLAIRE ZACHANASSIAN   This *is* Güllen, Moby. I recognize the pathetic little dump. Over there are the woods of

Konradsweil with the brook, where you can go fishing—trout and pike. And that roof on the right is Petersen's barn.

ILL (*as if awakening*) Clara.

TEACHER It's Zachanassian.

ALL Zachanassian.

TEACHER And the mixed choir isn't ready, the youth club!

MAYOR The gymnasts, the fire department!

PASTOR The sexton!

MAYOR My frock coat, for God's sake, my top hat, my grandchildren!

FIRST MAN Clairie Wäscher's here! Clairie Wäscher's here! (*He jumps up and rushes off toward town.*)

MAYOR (*calling after him*) Don't forget my wife!

TRAIN SUPERVISOR I am waiting for an explanation. Officially. In the name of the Railway Authorities.

CLAIRE ZACHANASSIAN You are a blockhead. I'm here to pay this little town a visit. Do you expect me to jump off your express train at full speed?

TRAIN SUPERVISOR Madam, if you wish to visit the town of Güllen, please, the twelve-forty local from Kalberstadt is at your service. At everyone's service. Arrival in Güllen one thirteen p.m.

CLAIRE ZACHANASSIAN You mean the local that stops in Loken, Brunnhübel, Beisenbach, and Leuthenau? You really expect me to go puffing around the countryside for half an hour?

TRAIN SUPERVISOR Madam, this will cost you dearly.

CLAIRE ZACHANASSIAN Give him a thousand, Boby.

ALL (*murmuring*) A thousand.

The Butler gives the Train Supervisor a thousand.

TRAIN SUPERVISOR (*baffled*) Madam.

CLAIRE ZACHANASSIAN And three thousand for the Railway Widows' Relief Fund.

ALL (*murmuring*) Three thousand.

The Train Supervisor receives three thousand from the Butler.

TRAIN SUPERVISOR (*bewildered*) There is no such relief fund, Madam.

CLAIRE ZACHANASSIAN Then start one.

The Mayor whispers something in the Train Supervisor's ear.

TRAIN SUPERVISOR (*dismayed*) Madam is Madam Claire Zachanassian? Oh, I beg your pardon. That is a different matter, of course. We certainly would have stopped in Güllen if we'd had the faintest idea—here is your money back, Madam—four thousand—my God.

ALL (*murmuring*) Four thousand.

CLAIRE ZACHANASSIAN Keep it, it's nothing.

ALL (*murmuring*) Keep it.

TRAIN SUPERVISOR Would Madam prefer the "Racing Roland" to wait while she visits Güllen? The railway management would gladly comply. The portal of the cathedral is said to be remarkable. Gothic. With the Last Judgment.

CLAIRE ZACHANASSIAN Just zoom off, you and your train.

11

HUSBAND VII (*whining*)   But the media, sweetie, the media people didn't get off yet. The reporters have no idea; they're dining up front in the dining car.

CLAIRE ZACHANASSIAN   Let them dine, Moby. I don't need the media in Güllen just yet. They'll come soon enough.

Meanwhile the Second Man has brought the Mayor his frock coat. The Mayor approaches Claire Zachanassian with a ceremonious air. The Painter and the Fourth Man on the bench raise their banner: "Welcome Claire Zachanassi . . ." The painter didn't quite finish it.

STATION MASTER (*raising his baton*)   Stand clear!

TRAIN SUPERVISOR   I sincerely hope Madam does not complain to the railway management. It was a pure misunderstanding.

The train starts moving. The Train Supervisor jumps on.

MAYOR   Dear Madam Zachanassian. As mayor of Güllen, it is my honor to welcome you, a child of our town . . .

The Mayor goes on talking, though the rest of his speech is obliterated by the din of the train as it races away.

CLAIRE ZACHANASSIAN   Thank you, Mayor, for your beautiful speech.

She approaches Ill, who has stepped toward her, somewhat embarrassed.

ILL   Clara.

CLAIRE ZACHANASSIAN   Alfred.

ILL   How nice that you came.

CLAIRE ZACHANASSIAN   It's something I always planned to do. All my life, ever since I left Güllen.

ILL (*unsure of himself*)   That's sweet of you.

CLAIRE ZACHANASSIAN   You thought about me too?

ILL   Of course. Always. You know I did, Clara.

CLAIRE ZACHANASSIAN   That was a wonderful time, all the days we spent together.

ILL (*proudly*)   You bet. (*to the teacher*)   You see, my dear teacher, I've got her in the bag.

CLAIRE ZACHANASSIAN   Call me what you always used to call me.

ILL   My little wildcat.

CLAIRE ZACHANASSIAN (*purring like an old cat*)   And what else?

ILL   My little sorceress.

CLAIRE ZACHANASSIAN   I called you my black panther.

ILL   I still am.

CLAIRE ZACHANASSIAN   Nonsense. You've gotten fat and gray and you look like a drunk.

ILL   But you've remained the same. My little sorceress.

CLAIRE ZACHANASSIAN   Oh, phooey. I've gotten old too, and fat. And my left leg is gone. A car accident. Now I only travel in express trains. But the artificial one is quite something, don't you think? (*She raises her skirt and shows her left leg.*)   It moves nicely.

ILL (*mops his brow*)   I would never have guessed, my little wildcat.

13

CLAIRE ZACHANASSIAN   May I introduce you to my seventh husband, Alfred? He owns tobacco plantations. We're happily married.

ILL   Oh, certainly.

CLAIRE ZACHANASSIAN   Come, Moby, make a bow. Actually his real name is Pedro, but Moby sounds better. Also, it goes well with Boby, my butler's name. Butlers are with you for life, so my husbands have to adapt their names to his.

Husband VII bows.

CLAIRE ZACHANASSIAN *(cont.)*   Isn't he cute with his black moustache? Think, Moby.

Husband VII thinks.

CLAIRE ZACHANASSIAN *(cont.)*   Harder.

Husband VII thinks harder.

CLAIRE ZACHANASSIAN *(cont.)*   Even harder.

HUSBAND VII   But I can't think any harder than that, my buttercup, really.

CLAIRE ZACHANASSIAN   Sure you can. Just try.

Husband VII thinks even harder.

Bell rings.

CLAIRE ZACHANASSIAN *(cont.)*   You see, it worked. He looks almost demonic this way, doesn't he, Alfred? Like a Brazilian. But he isn't at all. He's Greek Orthodox. His father was Russian. We were married by a Greek Orthodox priest. Fascinating. Now I'm going to have a look around Güllen. (*She inspects the little house on her left through a jewel-* .

14

studded lorgnette.)   My father built this public convenience, Moby. Good work, precisely executed. As a child, I used to sit on the roof for hours, spitting. But only on the men.

The mixed choir and the Youth Club have now assembled upstage. The Teacher steps forward wearing a top hat.

TEACHER   Madam, as Headmaster of Güllen High School and lover of the noble muse of music, may I take the liberty of offering you a simple folk song, presented by the mixed choir and the Youth Club.

CLAIRE ZACHANASSIAN   Shoot, teacher, let's hear your simple folk song.

The Teacher takes out a tuning fork, strikes it, the mixed choir and Youth Club start singing solemnly, but at this moment a new train arrives from the left. The Stationmaster salutes. The choir struggles against the clattering of the train, the teacher despairs, finally the train passes.

MAYOR (*disconsolate*)   The fire bell, they were supposed to sound the fire bell!

CLAIRE ZACHANASSIAN   Well sung, Gülleners. Especially that blond bass on the left, with the big Adam's apple, was remarkable.

A POLICEMAN pushes his way through the mixed choir, walks up to Claire Zachanassian, and stands at attention.

POLICEMAN   Officer Hahncke, Madam. At your service.

CLAIRE ZACHANASSIAN (*inspects him*)   Thanks. I don't intend to arrest anyone. But perhaps Güllen will have need of you. Do you sometimes turn a blind eye?

POLICEMAN   I do, Madam. How else could I get by in Güllen?

15

CLAIRE ZACHANASSIAN Might as well shut both your eyes from now on.

The Policeman stands there somewhat dumbfounded.

ILL *(laughs)* That's my Clara! That's my little sorceress! *(He slaps his thigh with pleasure.)*

The Mayor dons the teacher's top hat and presents his two grandchildren. Twins, seven years old, blonde braids.

MAYOR My grandchildren, Madam, Hermione and Adolfine. Only my wife is missing. *(He mops his brow.)*

The two little girls curtsy and offer Claire Zachanassian red roses.

CLAIRE ZACHANASSIAN Congrats on your brats, Mayor. There! *(She dumps the roses into the Stationmaster's arms.)*

The Mayor secretly hands the top hat to the Pastor, who puts it on.

MAYOR Our pastor, Madam.

The Pastor tips the top hat, bows.

CLAIRE ZACHANASSIAN Ah, the pastor. Do you comfort the dying?

PASTOR *(surprised)* I try to.

CLAIRE ZACHANASSIAN Does that include people who have been sentenced to death?

PASTOR *(confused)* The death sentence has been abolished in our country, Madam.

CLAIRE ZACHANASSIAN It could be reintroduced.

Somewhat dismayed, the Pastor hands the top hat back to the Mayor, who puts it back on his head. DOCTOR NÜSSLIN pushes his way through the crowd.

MAYOR Doctor Nüsslin, our physician.

CLAIRE ZACHANASSIAN Interesting. Do you prepare death certificates?

DOCTOR Death certificates?

CLAIRE ZACHANASSIAN When someone loses his life.

DOCTOR Yes, I do.

CLAIRE ZACHANASSIAN Next time you determine the cause of death, call it a heart attack.

ILL (*laughing*) My little wildcat! What hilarious jokes you make!

CLAIRE ZACHANASSIAN Now I want to go into town.

The Mayor wants to offer his arm.

CLAIRE ZACHANASSIAN (*cont.*) Mayor, do you really expect me to hike for miles with my artificial leg?

MAYOR (*shocked*) Right away! Right away! Doctor Nüsslin has a car.

DOCTOR A nineteen thirty-two Mercedes, Madam.

CLAIRE ZACHANASSIAN No need. Since my accident I only move around in a sedan chair. Roby and Toby, go and get it.

Two herculean, gum-chewing brutes enter left with a sedan chair. One of them has a guitar slung over his back.

CLAIRE ZACHANASSIAN (*cont.*) Two gangsters from Manhattan, sentenced to die in the electric chair at Sing Sing. Released at my request to carry my sedan chair. One million dollars per petition is what it cost me. The sedan chair comes from the Louvre, a gift from the French

17

president. A nice gentleman. Looks just like he does in the papers. Carry me into the town, Roby and Toby.

ROBY AND TOBY Yes, Ma'am.

CLAIRE ZACHANASSIAN But first to Petersen's barn, and then to the woods of Konradsweil. I want to visit our old trysting places with Alfred. In the meantime, take the luggage and the coffin to the Golden Apostle.

MAYOR (*startled*) The coffin?

CLAIRE ZACHANASSIAN I brought one along. I may need it. Go ahead, Roby and Toby.

The two gum-chewing brutes carry Claire Zachanassian to the town. The mayor gives a sign, and all burst into cheers, which, however, are dampened by bafflement when two servants enter, bearing a sumptuous black coffin, and carry it off to Güllen. But at this moment the fire bell (not pawned yet) starts ringing.

MAYOR At last! The fire bell!

The townspeople gather around the coffin. Claire Zachanassian's maidservants follow with the baggage and an interminable series of trunks, which are carried by the Gülleners. The Policeman directs this traffic, wants to follow the procession, but at that point two small, fat, old men enter, right, holding hands, both neatly dressed.

THE PAIR We're in Güllen. We can smell it, we can smell it, we can smell it in the air, the Güllen air.

POLICEMAN And who are you?

THE PAIR We belong to the old lady, we belong to the old lady. She calls us Koby and Loby.

POLICEMAN Madam Zachanassian is lodging at the Golden Apostle.

THE PAIR (*cheerfully*)   We are blind, we are blind.

POLICEMAN   Blind? Then I'll take the two of you there.

THE PAIR   Thank you, Mr. Policeman, thank you very much.

POLICEMAN (*surprised*)   How do you know I'm a policeman if you're blind?

THE PAIR   By the tone of your voice, by the tone of your voice, all policemen have the same tone of voice.

POLICEMAN (*suspiciously*)   You seem to have had some dealings with the police, you fat little men.

THE PAIR (*astonished*)   Men, he thinks we're men!

POLICEMAN   If you're not men, what the hell are you?

THE PAIR   You'll figure it out, you'll figure it out!

POLICEMAN (*baffled*)   Well, at least you're always cheerful.

THE PAIR   We get cutlets and ham. Every day, every day.

POLICEMAN   I'd do a little jig for that too. Come on, give me your hands. Funny sense of humor they've got. Foreigners. (*Goes off to the town with the Pair.*)

THE PAIR   Off to Boby and Moby, off to Roby and Toby!

Scenery change without curtain. The facades of the station and the little house rise and disappear. Interior of the Golden Apostle. A hotel sign could be let down from above, perhaps a gilded emblem representing a venerable apostle, and remain suspended in the center of the stage. The ruins of a bygone luxury: everything threadbare, dusty, moldy, cracked, and tattered, with crumbling plaster everywhere. The Mayor, the Pastor, and the Teacher are seated in the foreground on the right, drinking schnapps, and watching the endless procession of porters with trunks and valises, a sight that is left to the audience's imagination.

MAYOR   Suitcases, nothing but suitcases.

PASTOR   Loads of them. And a while ago they carried a panther upstairs in a cage.

MAYOR   A wild black beast.

PASTOR   The coffin.

MAYOR   Goes to a room of its own.

TEACHER   Strange.

PASTOR   World-famous ladies have their whims.

MAYOR   Pretty chambermaids.

TEACHER   It seems she plans to stay a while.

MAYOR   So much the better. Ill has her in the bag. His little wildcat, his little sorceress he called her. He'll get millions out of her. To your health, sir. To the chance that Claire Zachanassian will put Bockmann & Co. back on its feet again.

TEACHER   The Wagner Works.

MAYOR   The Hopewell Foundry. Once that gets going, everything else will: our community, our high school, our standard of living.

They clink glasses.

TEACHER   For more than two decades I've been correcting our students' Latin and Greek exercises, Your Honor, but only in this past hour have I learned the true meaning of horror. Seeing that old lady stepping out of the train in her black

20

robes made my hair stand on end. Like one of the Fates, like an avenging goddess. Her name should be Clotho, not Claire. I could well imagine her spinning the web of destiny.

The Policeman enters, hangs his helmet on a hook.

MAYOR Pull up a chair, Officer.

The Policeman pulls up a chair.

POLICEMAN It's not much fun working in this dump. But now new life will sprout from the ruin. I've just been to Petersen's barn with the billionairess and the shopkeeper, Ill. A touching scene. Both of them standing all solemn, like in a church. Embarrassing for me to watch them. So I stayed away when they went to the woods of Konradsweil. A regular procession. Two fat blind men in front with the butler, then the sedan chair, and behind it Ill and her seventh husband with his fishing gear.

MAYOR She's a man-eater.

TEACHER A second Laïs.

PASTOR We are all sinners.

MAYOR I wonder what they're after in the woods of Konradsweil.

POLICEMAN The same as in Petersen's barn, Your Honor. They're visiting the localities where their passion once— what's the word—

PASTOR Burned!

TEACHER Blazed is more like it! Reminds one of Shakespeare. Romeo and Juliet. Gentlemen: I am deeply stirred. For the first time in Güllen I feel the greatness of antiquity.

MAYOR Above all, let us drink to our good friend Ill, who is doing everything he possibly can to improve our lot. Gentlemen, to our most popular citizen, to my successor!

They clink glasses.

MAYOR (*cont.*) More suitcases.

POLICEMAN What a lot of luggage.

The Apostle sign rises up again. Enter the four citizens, left, with a simple, backless wooden bench, which they set down on the left. The First Man, around his neck a large cardboard heart with the inscription A+C, climbs onto the bench. The others stand around him in a half circle, with outspread arms holding twigs to represent trees.

FIRST MAN We are pine trees, hawthorn, oaks.

SECOND MAN We are beech and spruce and willow.

THIRD MAN Moss and lichen, ivy thickets.

FOURTH MAN Undergrowth and fox's lair.

FIRST MAN German woodland's wild profusion.

SECOND MAN Drifting clouds and cries of birds.

THIRD MAN Timid deer and magic mushrooms.

FOURTH MAN Whispering branches, ancient dreams.

The two gum-chewing brutes emerge from upstage, carrying Claire Zachanassian on the sedan chair, Ill at her side. Behind her, Husband VII. In the distant background, the Butler, leading the two blind men by the hand.

CLAIRE ZACHANASSIAN The woods of Konradsweil. Roby and Toby, stop for a moment.

THE PAIR Stop, Roby and Toby, stop, Boby and Moby.

Claire Zachanassian descends from the sedan chair, looks at the forest.

CLAIRE ZACHANASSIAN The heart with our names, Alfred, yours and mine. Almost faded away and the letters have moved apart. The tree has grown, its trunk, its branches have grown heavier, like our bodies. (*She goes to the other trees.*) German woodland. It's been a long time since I walked through the woods of my youth, tramping through the leaves, through the purple ivy. You two go chew your gum behind those bushes, and take the sedan chair with you; I'm tired of your faces. And you, Moby, go wander over to that brook on the right, you'll find your fish there.

The two brutes exit, left, with the sedan chair. Husband VII exits right. Claire Zachanassian sits down on the bench.

CLAIRE ZACHANASSIAN Look, a deer.

Third Man bounds off.

ILL It's the close season. (*He sits down next to her.*)

CLAIRE ZACHANASSIAN We kissed on this boulder. More than forty-five years ago. We made love under these bushes, under this beech tree, among toadstools on the moss. I was seventeen and you weren't quite twenty. Then you married Matilda Blumhard with her general store and I married old Zachanassian with his billions from Armenia. He found me in a Hamburg brothel. It was my red hair that attracted him to me, that golden old June bug.

ILL Clara!

CLAIRE ZACHANASSIAN A Henry Clay, Boby.

THE PAIR A Henry Clay, a Henry Clay.

The Butler comes from upstage, passes her a cigar, lights it.

CLAIRE ZACHANASSIAN   I enjoy cigars. I suppose I should smoke my husband's, but I don't trust them.

ILL   It was for your sake I married Matilda Blumhard.

CLAIRE ZACHANASSIAN   She had money.

ILL   You were young and beautiful. The future belonged to you. I wanted your happiness. So I had to renounce my own.

CLAIRE ZACHANASSIAN   Now the future has come.

ILL   If you had stayed here, you would have been as ruined as I am.

CLAIRE ZACHANASSIAN   You're ruined?

ILL   A bankrupt shopkeeper in a bankrupt town.

CLAIRE ZACHANASSIAN   Now I have money.

ILL   I've been living in hell since you left me.

CLAIRE ZACHANASSIAN   And I have become hell itself.

ILL   It's a constant fight with my family. Every day they blame me for being poor.

CLAIRE ZACHANASSIAN   Little Matilda didn't make you happy?

ILL   The main thing is that you're happy.

CLAIRE ZACHANASSIAN   Your children?

ILL   No sense of ideals.

CLAIRE ZACHANASSIAN   Don't worry, that'll come.

He falls silent. They both gaze at the woods of their youth.

24

ILL   I'm leading a ridiculous life. I never even managed to really leave this town. One trip to Berlin and another one to Tessin, that's all.

CLAIRE ZACHANASSIAN   Why bother, anyway. I know the world.

ILL   Because you could always travel.

CLAIRE ZACHANASSIAN   Because I own it.

He says nothing, and she smokes.

ILL   Now everything will be different.

CLAIRE ZACHANASSIAN   Definitely.

ILL (*with a wily look*)   You're going to help us?

CLAIRE ZACHANASSIAN   I won't abandon the town of my youth.

ILL   We need millions.

CLAIRE ZACHANASSIAN   That's not much.

ILL (*enthusiastically*)   My little wildcat! (*Moved, he slaps her left thigh and immediately withdraws his hand, wincing with pain.*)

CLAIRE ZACHANASSIAN   That hurts. You hit one of the hinges on my artificial leg.

The First Man pulls an old pipe and a rusty key from his pants pocket, knocks against the pipe with the key.

CLAIRE ZACHANASSIAN (*cont.*)   A woodpecker.

ILL   It's just like it was when we were young and bold, when we went out walking in the woods of Konradsweil, in the days of our love. The sun high above the pines, a bright disk. Drifting cloud banks in the distance and the cry of the cuckoo somewhere in the woody wilderness.

FOURTH MAN   Cuckoo! Cuckoo!

ILL (*feeling the First Man with his hand*)   Cool wood and wind in the branches, roaring and sighing like surf on the beach. Just like it used to be. Just like it was.

The three men representing trees make a whooshing sound, waving their arms up and down.

ILL (*cont.*)   I wish time were suspended, my little sorceress. If only life hadn't torn us apart.

CLAIRE ZACHANASSIAN   You wish that?

ILL   Just that, nothing else. You know I love you! (*He kisses her right hand.*)   The same cool white hand.

CLAIRE ZACHANASSIAN   You're wrong. Another prosthesis. Ivory.

ILL (*dropping her hand, horrified*)   Clara, is everything about you artificial?!

CLAIRE ZACHANASSIAN   Almost. From a plane crash in Afghanistan. I was the only one who crawled out of the wreckage. I'm indestructible.

THE PAIR   Indestructible, indestructible.

Solemn brass music. The hotel apostle descends again. Gülleners bring in tables covered with wretchedly tattered tablecloths, cutlery, and food. One table in the middle, one on the left, one on the right, parallel to the audience. The Pastor emerges from upstage. More Gülleners come streaming in, among them a man in a gymnast's outfit. The Mayor, the Doctor, the Teacher, and the Policeman reappear. The Gülleners applaud. The Mayor goes to the bench where Claire Zachanassian and Ill are sitting. The trees have turned into citizens again and have moved upstage.

MAYOR   The storm of applause was for you, my dear lady.

CLAIRE ZACHANASSIAN   It's for the town band, Mayor. They blow their instruments very well indeed, and the Gymnast's Club made a beautiful pyramid before.

The Mayor signals with his hand, and the GYMNAST presents himself to all.

CLAIRE ZACHANASSIAN (*cont.*)   I love men in undershirts and short pants. They look so natural. Do another exercise. Swing your arms back, young man, and then do some push-ups.

The Gymnast follows her instructions.

CLAIRE ZACHANASSIAN (*cont.*)   Marvelous muscles! Have you ever used your strength to strangle someone?

The Gymnast halts in mid-push-up, astonished, and sinks to his knees.

GYMNAST   Strangle?

ILL (*laughing*)   What a golden sense of humor Clara has! Her jokes just kill me!

DOCTOR   I don't know. I find them rather chilling.

Gymnast exits upstage.

MAYOR   May I escort you to the table? (*He escorts Claire Zachanassian to the central table, introduces her to his wife.*)   My wife.

CLAIRE ZACHANASSIAN (*examines the wife through her lorgnette*) Annie Dummermut, top of our class.

Ill fetches his wife, a skinny, embittered woman.

CLAIRE ZACHANASSIAN (*cont.*)   Little Matilda Blumhard. I remember you lurking behind the shop door, on the lookout for Alfred. You've grown skinny and pale, my dear.

ILL (*aside*)   She's promised millions!

MAYOR (*gasping*)   Millions?

ILL   Millions.

DOCTOR   Incredible.

CLAIRE ZACHANASSIAN   Now I'm hungry, Mayor.

MAYOR   We're just waiting for your husband, Madam.

CLAIRE ZACHANASSIAN   No need to wait. He's fishing, and I'm getting a divorce.

MAYOR   A divorce?

CLAIRE ZACHANASSIAN   Moby will be surprised too. I'm marrying a German film star.

MAYOR   But you said your marriage was a happy one!

CLAIRE ZACHANASSIAN   Every one of my marriages is happy. But it was the dream of my youth to be wed in the Güllen Cathedral. And the dreams of one's youth must be realized. It'll be a most solemn occasion.

All sit down. Claire Zachanassian sits between the Mayor and Ill. Mrs. Ill sits next to Ill, the Mayor's wife next to the Mayor. On the right behind another table sit the Teacher, the Pastor, and the Policeman. On the left, the Four Men. Further guests of honor with their wives in the background. There, too, is the illuminated banner: WELCOME CLAIRIE. The Mayor stands up, beaming with pleasure, a napkin already tied around his neck, and knocks his spoon against his glass.

MAYOR   Dear Madam, my dear fellow Gülleners. It was forty-five years ago that you left our little town, founded by

28

the Elector Hasso the Noble, so pleasantly ensconced between the woods of Konradsweil and Pückenried Valley. Forty-five years, more than four decades, a lot of time. Much has happened since, many bitter events. The world has taken a sad turn, and so have we. And yet we have never forgotten you, dear Madam—our Clairie (*applause*)   —nor have we forgotten your family. Your splendid mother, so robust and healthy, so deeply fulfilled by her marriage and—(*Ill whispers something to him*)   —but alas, prematurely torn from our midst; your father, truly a man of the people, who erected a building next to the station that attracts large numbers of laymen and experts alike (*Ill whispers something to him*)   visitors, that is; both your parents still live on in our memory as the best, the most worthy among us. And above all you, my dear lady, frolicking through our streets as a blonde (*Ill whispers something to him*) redheaded tomboy—streets that today are, alas, in such sad disrepair—was there anyone who did not know you? Even then everyone could sense the charm of your personality, could sense your eventual rise to the dizzying heights of humanity. (*He pulls out his notebook.*)   You have remained unforgettable. Truly. Your academic achievements are still held up as an example by our educators, especially the interest you showed in the most important subject, botany and zoology, thus expressing your sympathy with every living being, indeed with all creatures in need of protection. Even then, your love of justice and your charitable nature were widely admired. (*Tremendous applause.*)   Was it not our Clairie who obtained food for a poor old widow by purchasing potatoes with pocket money she had earned by working for neighbors, thus saving the life of an old woman who would otherwise have died of hunger, to mention just one of her errands of mercy? (*Tremendous applause.*)   Dear Madam, dear Gülleners, the tender seeds of these promising instincts have now come to full bloom, our little redheaded tomboy has turned into a lady whose charity embraces the whole world. We need only think of her social welfare endowments, her maternity homes and soup kitchens, her art foundations and kindergartens, and so I want to call out to our beloved prodigal daughter who at last has found her way home: Hurrah! Hurrah! Hurrah!

Applause. Claire Zachanassian rises.

CLAIRE ZACHANASSIAN Mayor, Gülleners. I am touched by your unselfish display of joy over my visit. As a matter of fact, I was a rather different child from the one described in the mayor's speech. I was beaten in school, and I stole those potatoes for the widow Boll, together with Ill, not to save the old panderer from dying of hunger, but just to have a chance for once to lie with Ill in a bed, where it was more comfortable than in the woods of Konradsweil or Petersen's barn. But as my contribution to your joy, I want to tell you right now that I am prepared to give Güllen a present of one billion. Five hundred million to the town and five hundred million divided among all the families.

Deathly silence.

MAYOR *(stammering)* One billion.

Everyone still petrified.

CLAIRE ZACHANASSIAN On one condition.

Everyone bursts into indescribable jubilation, dancing about, standing on chairs, the Gymnast doing gymnastics, and so on. Ill thumps his chest enthusiastically.

ILL That's Clara! Pure gold! Wonderful! She's a riot! My little sorceress through and through! (*He kisses her.*)

30

MAYOR   On one condition, you said, dear Madam. May I ask: on what condition?

CLAIRE ZACHANASSIAN   I will tell you the condition. I will give you a billion, and with that billion I will buy myself justice.

Deathly silence.

MAYOR   What exactly do you mean by that, Madam?

CLAIRE ZACHANASSIAN   I mean what I said.

MAYOR   But justice can't be bought!

CLAIRE ZACHANASSIAN   Everything can be bought.

MAYOR   I still don't understand.

CLAIRE ZACHANASSIAN   Step forward, Boby.

The Butler moves from the right to the center between the three tables, takes off his dark glasses.

BUTLER   I don't know if any of you still recognize me.

TEACHER   Chief Justice Hofer.

BUTLER   Correct. Chief Justice Hofer. Forty-five years ago I was Chief Justice of Güllen and then moved on to the Court of Appeal in Kaffigen, until twenty-five years ago Mrs. Zachanassian offered me the opportunity to enter her service as her butler. I accepted. A peculiar career for a man of learning, perhaps, but the salary was so fantastic—

CLAIRE ZACHANASSIAN   Get to the point, Boby.

BUTLER   As you have heard, Mrs. Claire Zachanassian is offering a billion and wants justice in return. In other words: Mrs. Claire Zachanassian is offering a billion

31

provided you make amends for the wrong that was done to Mrs. Zachanassian in Güllen. Mr. Ill, if you please.

Ill stands, pale, at once frightened and puzzled.

ILL What do you want from me?

BUTLER Step forward, Mr. Ill.

ILL All right. (*He steps forward to the table on the right. Laughs uncomfortably. Shrugs.*)

BUTLER The year was nineteen ten. I was Chief Justice in Güllen and had a paternity claim to arbitrate. Claire Zachanassian, Clara Wäscher at the time, charged you with being the father of her child.

Ill says nothing.

BUTLER (*cont.*) You denied paternity, Mr. Ill. You had brought along two witnesses.

ILL This happened long ago. I was young and heedless.

CLAIRE ZACHANASSIAN Toby and Roby, bring in Koby and Loby.

The two gum-chewing brutes lead the two blind, cheerfully hand-holding eunuchs to the center of the stage.

THE PAIR At your service, at your service!

BUTLER Do you recognize these two, Mr. Ill?

Ill remains silent.

THE PAIR We are Koby and Loby, we are Koby and Loby.

ILL I don't know them.

THE PAIR We have changed, we have changed.

BUTLER Say your names.

THE FIRST ONE Jakob Duckling, Jakob Duckling.

THE SECOND ONE Walter Perch, Walter Perch.

BUTLER Well, Mr. Ill?

ILL I know nothing about them.

BUTLER Jakob Duckling, Walter Perch, do you know Mr. Ill?

THE PAIR We are blind, we are blind.

BUTLER Do you know him by his voice?

THE PAIR By his voice, by his voice.

BUTLER In nineteen ten I was the judge and you were the witnesses. What did you swear, Walter Perch and Jakob Duckling, before the court in Güllen?

THE PAIR That we had slept with Clara, that we had slept with Clara.

BUTLER That's what you swore before me. Before the court, before God. Was this the truth?

THE PAIR We swore falsely, we swore falsely.

BUTLER Why, Walter Perch and Jakob Duckling?

THE PAIR Ill bribed us, Ill bribed us.

BUTLER With what?

THE PAIR With a quart of schnapps, with a quart of schnapps.

CLAIRE ZACHANASSIAN Now tell them what I did with you, Koby and Loby.

33

BUTLER   Tell them.

THE PAIR   The lady tracked us down, the lady tracked us down.

BUTLER   That's right. Claire Zachanassian tracked you down. Sent out search parties for you all over the world. Jakob Duckling had emigrated to Canada, Walter Perch to Australia. But she found you. And what did she do with you then?

THE PAIR   She gave us to Toby and Roby. She gave us to Toby and Roby.

BUTLER   And what did Toby and Roby do to you?

THE PAIR   Castrated and blinded us, castrated and blinded us.

BUTLER   That's the story: A judge, a defendant, two false witnesses, a miscarriage of justice in the year nineteen ten. Is that not so, plaintiff?

Claire Zachanassian stands up.

ILL (*stamping the floor*)   Ancient history! It's just a crazy old story!

BUTLER   What happened to the child, plaintiff?

CLAIRE ZACHANASSIAN (*softly*)   It lived for a year.

BUTLER   What happened to you?

CLAIRE ZACHANASSIAN   I became a prostitute.

BUTLER   Why?

CLAIRE ZACHANASSIAN   The court's verdict turned me into one.

BUTLER   And now you want justice, Claire Zachanassian?

34

CLAIRE ZACHANASSIAN   I can afford justice. One billion for Güllen, if someone kills Alfred Ill.

Deathly silence.

MRS. ILL (*rushes to Ill, throws her arms around him*)   Freddy!

ILL   My little sorceress! You can't ask for that! Life has gone on since then!

CLAIRE ZACHANASSIAN   Life has gone on, but I have forgotten nothing, Ill. Neither the woods of Konradsweil nor Petersen's barn, neither Widow Boll's bedroom nor your treachery. Now we have grown old, the two of us, you down at the heels and me cut to pieces by surgeons' knives, and now I want us both to settle accounts: you chose your life and forced me into mine. You wanted time to be suspended, just a moment ago, in the woods of our youth, so full of impermanence. Now I have suspended it, and now I want justice, justice for a billion.

The Mayor stands up, pale, dignified.

MAYOR   Mrs. Zachanassian, we are still in Europe; we're not savages yet. In the name of the town of Güllen I reject your offer. In the name of humanity. We would rather be poor than have blood on our hands.

Tremendous applause.

CLAIRE ZACHANASSIAN   I can wait.

35

ACT TWO

The small town—just a bare indication of it. In the background the exterior of the Golden Apostle Hotel. Dilapidated art nouveau facade. Balcony. On the right a sign: ALFRED ILL, GENERAL STORE. *Beneath it a dirty counter, behind that a shelf with old merchandise. Whenever someone enters through the imaginary door, a bell tinkles. On the left a sign:* POLICE. *Beneath it a wooden table with a telephone. Two chairs. It is morning. Roby and Toby enter, left, chewing gum, carrying wreaths and flowers as though in preparation for a funeral, and cross the stage toward the back and into the hotel. Ill watches them through the window. His* DAUGHTER *is sweeping the floor on her knees. His* SON *puts a cigarette in his mouth.*

ILL Wreaths.

SON Every morning they bring them from the station.

ILL For the empty coffin in the Golden Apostle.

SON Doesn't scare anyone.

ILL The town is on my side.

The Son lights the cigarette.

ILL (*cont.*) Is Mother coming down for breakfast?

DAUGHTER She's staying upstairs. Says she's tired.

ILL You have a good mother, children. I have to say it for once. A good mother. Let her stay upstairs, let her rest and take it easy. We'll have breakfast together, just the three of us. We haven't done that in a long time. I'll contribute some eggs and a can of American ham. Let's live it up. Like

36

in the good old days, when the Hopewell Foundry was thriving.

SON   You'll have to excuse me. (*He extinguishes his cigarette.*)

ILL   You don't want to eat with us, Karl?

SON   I'm going to the station. One of the workers is sick. Maybe they need a replacement.

ILL   Working on the railroad in the blazing sun, that's no job for my boy.

SON   Better than no job at all. (*He leaves.*)

DAUGHTER (*standing up*)   I'm leaving too, father.

ILL   You too. Hm. May I ask where you're going, young lady?

DAUGHTER   To the Employment Office. Maybe they have an opening. (*She leaves.*)

ILL (*moved, blows his nose*)   Good children, fine kids.

A few bars of guitar music coming from the balcony.

CLAIRE ZACHANASSIAN'S VOICE   Hand me my left leg, Boby.

BUTLER'S VOICE   I can't find it.

CLAIRE ZACHANASSIAN'S VOICE   On the dresser, behind the flowers I received from my fiancé.

Ill's first customer comes in (First Man).

ILL   Good morning, Hofbauer.

FIRST MAN   Cigarettes.

ILL   The usual.

37

FIRST MAN   Not those, I want the green ones.

ILL   More expensive.

FIRST MAN   Charge it.

ILL   Since it's you, Hofbauer, and because we all have to stick together.

FIRST MAN   Someone's playing a guitar.

ILL   One of the gangsters from Sing Sing.

The Pair come out of the hotel, carrying fishing rods and other fishing gear.

THE PAIR   Good morning, Alfred, good morning.

ILL   Go to hell.

THE PAIR   We're going fishing, we're going fishing. (*They exit, left.*)

FIRST MAN   They're going to the Güllen brook.

ILL   With her husband's fishing rods. Her seventh.

FIRST MAN   I heard he's lost his tobacco plantations.

ILL   They belong to the billionairess as well.

FIRST MAN   But there's going to be a terrific wedding with her eighth. Yesterday they celebrated their engagement.

Claire Zachanassian appears in a dressing gown on the balcony upstage. She moves her right hand, her left leg. Sporadically, individual notes plucked on the guitar may accompany the balcony scene that follows, somewhat in the manner of an opera recitative; corresponding to the meaning of the words, now a waltz, then fragments of various national anthems, and so on.

CLAIRE ZACHANASSIAN   I'm reassembled. The Armenian folk tune, Roby.

Guitar music.

CLAIRE ZACHANASSIAN (*cont.*)   Zachanassian's favorite piece. He always wanted to hear it. Every morning. He had class, all right, that old tycoon with his tremendous fleet of oil tankers and his racing stables, and billions in the bank. A marriage like that was still worthwhile. A great teacher, a great dancer, a master of all sorts of devilry. I learned all his tricks.

Two women come. They give Ill milk cans.

FIRST WOMAN   Milk, Mr. Ill.

SECOND WOMAN   My can, Mr. Ill.

ILL   Good morning. A quart of milk for each of the ladies.

He opens a milk canister and is about to ladle milk.

FIRST WOMAN   Whole milk, Mr. Ill.

SECOND WOMAN   Two quarts of whole milk, Mr. Ill.

ILL   Whole milk. (*He opens another canister and ladles milk.*)

Claire Zachanassian inspects the morning through her lorgnette.

CLAIRE ZACHANASSIAN   A lovely autumn morning. Light mist in the streets, a silvery haze, and above that a violet-blue sky like the ones Count Holk liked to paint, my third one, the Foreign Minister. Took up painting on his holidays. Hideous pictures. (*She sits down with an awkward, elaborate effort.*)   The Count was altogether hideous.

FIRST WOMAN   And butter. Half a pound.

39

SECOND WOMAN   And white bread. Two large loaves.

ILL   Must have come into money, ladies.

THE TWO WOMEN   Charge it.

ILL   All for one and one for all.

FIRST WOMAN   Plus some chocolate for two twenty.

SECOND WOMAN   Four forty.

ILL   Charge that too?

FIRST WOMAN   That too.

SECOND WOMAN   We'll eat these here, Mr. Ill.

FIRST WOMAN   We like your shop best, Mr. Ill.

They sit down in the back of the store and eat chocolate.

CLAIRE ZACHANASSIAN   A Cohibas. I want to try my seventh husband's brand, now that we're divorced. Poor Moby, with his passion for fish. How sad he must be now, sitting in the train to Portugal. In Lisbon one of my oil tankers will take him along to Brazil.

The Butler hands her a cigar, gives her a light.

FIRST MAN   There she is, sitting on her balcony, puffing her cigar.

ILL   Always sinfully expensive brands.

FIRST MAN   Conspicuous consumption. In full view of destitute humanity. She ought to be ashamed of herself.

CLAIRE ZACHANASSIAN (*smoking*)   Curious. Not bad at all.

ILL   She miscalculated. I'm an old sinner, Hofbauer, who isn't? It was a mean trick I played on her as a kid, but the way they all rejected that offer, the Gülleners in the Golden Apostle, unanimously, despite our misery, that was the most beautiful moment of my life.

CLAIRE ZACHANASSIAN   Whiskey, Boby. Straight up.

A second customer comes, impoverished and in rags, like everyone else (Second Man).

SECOND MAN   Good morning. Going to be hot today.

FIRST MAN   This spell of good weather just goes on and on.

ILL   The customers I've had this morning. Usually there's no one for the longest time, and now, for the past few days, they're coming in droves.

FIRST MAN   It's because we stand by you. We stick by our Ill. Firm as a rock.

THE WOMEN (*eating chocolate*)   Firm as a rock, Mr. Ill.

SECOND MAN   After all, you're the most popular man in town.

FIRST MAN   The most important.

SECOND MAN   You'll be elected mayor in the spring.

FIRST MAN   That's dead certain.

THE WOMEN (*eating chocolate*)   Dead certain, Mr. Ill, dead certain.

SECOND MAN   Schnapps.

Ill reaches for something on the shelf.

The Butler serves whiskey.

CLAIRE ZACHANASSIAN   Wake the new one. I don't like it when my husbands sleep so long.

41

ILL Three ten.

SECOND MAN Not that one.

ILL That's what you always have.

SECOND MAN Cognac.

ILL That's twenty thirty-five. No one can afford that.

SECOND MAN A man deserves a treat now and then.

A nearly half-naked girl dashes across the stage, pursued by Toby.

FIRST WOMAN (*eating chocolate*) It's outrageous, the way Louise is carrying on.

SECOND WOMAN (*eating chocolate*) And she's engaged to that blond musician from Berthold-Schwartzstrasse.

Ill takes down the cognac.

ILL Cognac.

SECOND MAN And tobacco. For my pipe.

ILL All right.

SECOND MAN Imported.

Ill adds everything up.

HUSBAND VIII, *a movie star, tall, slender, red moustache, appears on the balcony, wearing a dressing gown. He can be played by the same actor as Husband VII.*

HUSBAND VIII Hopsi, isn't this marvelous: newly engaged and our first breakfast together. Like a dream. A little balcony, a rustling linden tree, the splashing of the town hall fountain, a few chickens running across the street, housewives chattering somewhere about their small cares, and behind the rooftops the spire of the cathedral!

CLAIRE ZACHANASSIAN   Sit down, Hoby, don't talk. I can see the landscape myself, and thinking is not your strong suit.

SECOND MAN   Now the husband's sitting up there too.

FIRST WOMAN (*eating chocolate*)   Her eighth.

SECOND WOMAN (*eating chocolate*)   Good-looking man, a movie star. My daughter saw him as a rustler in a Western.

FIRST WOMAN   And I saw him as a priest in a Graham Greene.

Claire Zachanassian is being kissed by Husband VIII. Guitar chord.

SECOND MAN   You can get anything for money. (*He spits.*)

FIRST MAN   Not from us. (*He bangs his fist on the table.*)

ILL   Twenty-three eighty.

SECOND MAN   Charge it.

ILL   I'll make an exception this week, but be sure to pay me on the first, when the welfare checks are due.

Second man goes to the door.

ILL (*cont.*)   Helmesberger!

He stops. Ill walks toward him.

ILL (*cont.*)   You've got new shoes. New yellow shoes.

SECOND MAN   So?

ILL (*looking at the First Man's feet*)   You, too, Hofbauer. You, too, are wearing new shoes. (*He looks at the women, walks over to them slowly, horrified.*)   You too. New yellow shoes. New yellow shoes.

43

FIRST MAN   I don't know what you're getting at.

SECOND MAN   We can't just keep walking around in the same old shoes.

ILL   New shoes. How could you buy new shoes?

THE WOMEN   We bought them on credit, Mr. Ill, we bought them on credit.

ILL   You bought them on credit. You bought from me on credit too. Better tobacco, better milk, cognac. Why are you suddenly getting credit in all the stores?

SECOND MAN   But you yourself are giving us credit.

ILL   How are you going to pay?

Silence. He starts throwing his merchandise at the customers. They all run away.

ILL (*cont.*)   How are you going to pay? How are you going to pay? How? How? (*He dashes off to the back.*)

HUSBAND VIII   The natives are restless.

CLAIRE ZACHANASSIAN   Small-town existence.

HUSBAND VIII   Seems to be trouble in the shop down there.

CLAIRE ZACHANASSIAN   They must be haggling over the price of meat.

Strong guitar chord. Husband VIII leaps up, horrified.

HUSBAND VIII   For God's sake, Hopsi! Did you hear that?

CLAIRE ZACHANASSIAN   The black panther. He hissed.

HUSBAND VIII (*puzzled*)   A black panther?

44

CLAIRE ZACHANASSIAN From the Pasha of Marrakech. A present. Walks around the vestibule next door. A large wicked cat with sparkling eyes.

The Policeman sits down at the table on the left. Drinks beer. He speaks slowly, ponderously. Ill comes from the back of the stage.

CLAIRE ZACHANASSIAN (*cont.*) You may serve, Boby.

POLICEMAN What do you want, Ill? Have a seat.

Ill remains standing.

POLICEMAN (*cont.*) You're trembling.

ILL I demand the arrest of Claire Zachanassian.

POLICEMAN (*stuffs his pipe, lights it with leisurely, unhurried movements*) Peculiar. Extremely peculiar.

The Butler serves breakfast, brings the mail.

ILL I demand it as the future mayor.

POLICEMAN (*puffing clouds of smoke*) You haven't been elected yet.

ILL Arrest the lady on the spot.

POLICEMAN You mean you want to bring charges against the lady. Whether she then gets arrested is for the police to decide. Has she broken a law?

ILL She's inciting the people of the town to kill me.

POLICEMAN And now I'm supposed to simply arrest her. (*Pours himself beer.*)

CLAIRE ZACHANASSIAN The mail. One from Ike. Nehru. They send congratulations.

ILL Your duty.

POLICEMAN Peculiar. Extremely peculiar. (*He drinks beer.*)

ILL It's perfectly natural.

POLICEMAN Dear Ill, it's not all that natural. Let's examine this case with a calm, level mind. The lady made a proposal to the town of Güllen: one billion in exchange for your— you know what I mean. That's a fact, I was there. But these are not sufficient grounds for the police to take action against Claire Zachanassian. We have to abide by the law.

ILL Incitement to murder.

POLICEMAN Now listen here, Ill. We can speak of incitement to murder only if the proposal to murder you is meant seriously. That's only logical.

ILL I agree.

POLICEMAN Precisely. Now, this proposal cannot be meant seriously, because the price of one billion is just too extreme, you have to admit that yourself. For something like this, people offer a thousand, maybe two thousand, definitely no more than that, you can bet your life on it, which again proves that the proposal wasn't meant seriously; and if it were meant seriously, the police could not take the lady seriously, because in that case she would be crazy. You understand?

ILL The proposal threatens me, Officer, whether the lady is crazy or not. That's only logical.

POLICEMAN Illogical. You can't be threatened by a proposal, only by the carrying out of a proposal. Show me one genuine attempt to carry out this proposal, for instance a man pointing a gun at you, and I'll be there faster than you can blink an eye. But the truth of the matter is that no one intends to carry out this proposal. On the contrary. The demonstration at the Golden Apostle was extremely impressive. Congratulations is all I can say. (*He drinks beer.*)

ILL   I'm not so sure, Officer.

POLICEMAN   Not so sure?

ILL   My customers are buying better milk, better bread, better cigarettes.

POLICEMAN   Be glad! Business is looking up. (*He drinks beer.*)

CLAIRE ZACHANASSIAN   Boby, arrange for all the Dupont shares to be bought.

ILL   Helmesberger came to buy cognac. He hasn't had a job for years and depends on the soup kitchen.

POLICEMAN   I'll have a taste of that cognac tonight. Helmesberger's invited me over. (*He drinks beer.*)

ILL   They're all wearing new shoes. New yellow shoes.

POLICEMAN   What do you have against new shoes? I'm wearing new shoes myself. (*He shows his feet.*)

ILL   You too.

POLICEMAN   There you have it.

ILL   Yellow ones too. And drinking Pilsner beer.

POLICEMAN   It's good.

ILL   You used to drink the local beer.

POLICEMAN   It was awful.

Radio music.

ILL Do you hear that?

POLICEMAN So?

ILL Music.

POLICEMAN The *Merry Widow*.

ILL A radio.

POLICEMAN It's Hagholzer next door. He should close the window. (*Makes a note in his little notebook.*)

ILL How did Hagholzer get a radio?

POLICEMAN That's his business.

ILL And you, Officer, how are you going to pay for your Pilsner and your new shoes?

POLICEMAN That's my business.

The telephone on the table rings. The Policeman picks up the receiver.

POLICEMAN (*cont.*) Güllen police.

CLAIRE ZACHANASSIAN Boby, call up the Russians and tell them I accept their offer.

POLICEMAN Okay. (*He hangs up.*)

ILL My customers, how are they going to pay?

POLICEMAN That doesn't concern the police. (*He stands up and takes a rifle from the back of the chair.*)

ILL But it concerns me. Because it's me they're going to use for payment.

POLICEMAN No one is threatening you. (*He begins to load the rifle.*)

48

ILL   The town's going into debt. Debt and prosperity are both on the rise. The higher the standard of living, the greater the need to kill me. So all the lady has to do is sit on her balcony, drink coffee, smoke cigars, and wait. Just wait.

POLICEMAN   You're imagining things.

ILL   You're all waiting. (*He pounds on the table.*)

POLICEMAN   You've had too much schnapps. (*He checks his rifle.*)   There, now it's loaded. Rest assured: the police are here to enforce respect for the law, to maintain order, to protect the private citizen. The police know their duty. If the faintest suspicion of a threat arises, we will step in, Mr. Ill, you can be sure of that.

ILL (*softly*)   Why do you have a gold tooth in your mouth, Officer?

POLICEMAN   What?

ILL   A gleaming new gold tooth.

POLICEMAN   Are you out of your mind?

Now Ill sees that the barrel of the gun is pointing at himself, and slowly raises his hands.

POLICEMAN (*cont.*)   I don't have time to debate with you about your hallucinations, man. I have to go. That screwy billionairess has lost her little lap-dog. The black panther. I have to hunt it down. The whole town has to hunt it down. (*He goes toward the back of the stage and off.*)

ILL   It's me you're hunting, me.

CLAIRE ZACHANASSIAN (*reading a letter*)   He's coming, the dress designer. My fifth husband, the most good-looking of

49

all my husbands. He still designs all my wedding gowns. A minuet, Roby.

Guitar plays a minuet.

HUSBAND VIII But your fifth was a surgeon.

CLAIRE ZACHANASSIAN My sixth. (*Opens another letter.*) From the owner of Western Railways.

HUSBAND VIII (*astonished*) I never heard of that one.

CLAIRE ZACHANASSIAN My fourth. Impoverished. His shares belong to me. Seduced him in Buckingham Palace. In the light of the full moon.

HUSBAND VIII But that was Lord Ishmael.

CLAIRE ZACHANASSIAN So it was. You're right, Hoby. I forgot all about him and his castle in Yorkshire. So this letter must be from my second. Met him in Cairo. We kissed beneath the Sphinx. Impressive evening. Another full moon. Curious: the moon was always full.

Change of scenery on the right. The legend "Town Hall" descends. The Third Man enters, carries off the cash register, and shifts the counter into a different position, where it can now be used as a desk. The Mayor enters. Puts a revolver on the table, sits down. Ill enters from the left. A blueprint hangs on the wall.

ILL I have to talk to you, Your Honor.

MAYOR Have a seat.

ILL Man to man. As your successor.

MAYOR Be my guest.

Ill stays standing, looks at the revolver.

MAYOR Madam Zachanassian's panther has escaped. It's climbing around in the cathedral. So we have to be armed.

ILL Sure.

MAYOR I've called up all the men who have weapons. The children are being kept in school.

ILL (*suspiciously*) Sounds like a major operation.

MAYOR Big game hunting.

Enter Butler.

BUTLER The president of the World Bank, Madam. Just flew in from New York.

CLAIRE ZACHANASSIAN I'm not available. Tell him to fly back.

MAYOR What's eating you? You don't have to mince words, just tell me.

ILL (*suspiciously*) That's a fine brand you're smoking.

MAYOR A Pegasus claro.

ILL Pretty expensive.

MAYOR But worth it.

ILL You used to smoke a different brand, Your Honor.

MAYOR Trotters.

ILL Cheaper.

MAYOR Much too strong.

ILL A new tie?

MAYOR Silk.

ILL And I suppose you bought new shoes too?

MAYOR I had a pair shipped in from Kalberstadt. That's funny, how did you know?

ILL This is why I've come to see you.

MAYOR What is the matter with you? You look pale. Are you sick?

ILL I'm scared.

MAYOR Scared?

ILL Prosperity is on the rise.

MAYOR That's news to me. I wish it were so.

ILL I demand official protection.

MAYOR Really. What for?

ILL Your Honor, you already know what for.

MAYOR Suspicious?

ILL A billion has been offered for my head.

MAYOR Approach the police.

ILL I've been to the police.

MAYOR That should have reassured you.

ILL There's a new gold tooth gleaming in the officer's mouth.

MAYOR You forget that you're in Güllen. A town with a humanist tradition. Goethe slept here. Brahms composed a quartet. These values impose an obligation.

A man enters, left, with a typewriter (Third Man).

MAN The new typewriter, Your Honor. A Remington.

MAYOR It's for the office.

Man exits, right.

MAYOR (*cont.*) We don't deserve your ingratitude. If you're unable to place any trust in our community, I pity you. I never expected to see this nihilistic streak in you. You seem to forget that we live under the rule of law.

The two blind men enter, left, with their fishing rods, holding hands.

THE PAIR The panther is loose, the panther is loose! (*Skipping*) We've heard him growling, we've heard him growling! (*They skip into the Golden Apostle.*) We're going to Hoby and Boby, to Toby and Roby. (*They exit upstage center.*)

ILL Then arrest the lady.

MAYOR Peculiar. Extremely peculiar.

ILL That's what the police officer said too.

MAYOR God knows the lady's actions aren't all that hard to understand. After all, you did bribe two fellows to commit perjury, and you did condemn a young girl to a life of naked misery.

ILL This naked misery amounts to several billions, Your Honor.

Silence.

MAYOR Let's talk honestly.

ILL I would appreciate that.

MAYOR Man to man, the way you wanted. You don't have the moral right to demand the arrest of this lady, nor is there any chance of your becoming mayor. I'm sorry to have to tell you this.

ILL Officially?

MAYOR On behalf of both parties.

ILL I understand.

He slowly goes to the window, turning his back to the Mayor, and stares out.

MAYOR The fact that we condemn the lady's proposal does not mean that we condone the crimes that led to this proposal. For a man to hold the mayor's office, he must meet certain moral requirements that you are no longer able to fulfill, you have to understand that. We will of course continue to show you the same high regard and the same friendship as always. That goes without saying.

Roby and Toby enter, left, with more wreaths and flowers, cross the stage, and disappear inside the Golden Apostle.

MAYOR *(cont.)* I think it's best if we pass over the whole affair in silence. I've also asked the *Güllen Herald* not to let any of it get into print.

ILL *(turning around)* They're already decorating my coffin, Mayor! Silence is too dangerous for me.

MAYOR But why, my dear Ill? You should be thankful we're leaving this whole nasty business cloaked in oblivion.

ILL If I speak, I'll still have a chance to escape.

MAYOR Now that's really too much! Who would be threatening you?

ILL One of you.

54

MAYOR (*rises to his feet*)   Whom are you suspecting? Tell me his name and I will investigate the case. Relentlessly.

ILL   Every one of you.

MAYOR   I protest in the name of our town against this libel. Solemnly.

ILL   No one wants to kill me, everyone hopes that someone will do it, and so at some point someone will.

MAYOR   You are seeing ghosts.

ILL   I see a blueprint on the wall. The new town hall? (*He taps a finger against the blueprint.*)

MAYOR   My God, I should hope we can still make plans.

ILL   You're already speculating on my death!

MAYOR   My dear fellow, if I, as a politician, no longer had the right to believe in a better future without having to contemplate a crime, rest assured that I would resign.

ILL   You have already condemned me to death.

MAYOR   Mr. Ill!

ILL (*softly*)   The blueprint proves it! Proves it!

CLAIRE ZACHANASSIAN   Onassis is coming. The duke and the duchess. Aga.

HUSBAND VIII   Ali too?

CLAIRE ZACHANASSIAN   The whole Riviera crowd.

HUSBAND VIII   Journalists?

CLAIRE ZACHANASSIAN   From all over the world. Whenever I marry, the press is always present. It needs me, and I need it. (*She opens another letter.*)   From Count Holk.

HUSBAND VIII   Hopsi, this is our first breakfast together. Do you really have to spend it reading letters from your former husbands?

CLAIRE ZACHANASSIAN   I want to keep track of them.

HUSBAND VIII (*dolefully*)   I have problems too. (*He rises to his feet, stares down at the town.*)

CLAIRE ZACHANASSIAN   Something wrong with your Porsche?

HUSBAND VIII   Small towns like this depress me. All right, the linden tree's rustling, birds are singing, the fountain is splashing, but they were already doing that half an hour ago. There's just nothing happening, neither in nature nor in the people, nothing but deep, untroubled peace, contentment, satiety, and comfort. No grandeur, no tragedy. None of the ethical calling of a great age.

Enter the Pastor, left, with a rifle slung around his shoulder. He spreads a white cloth with a black cross over the table where the Policeman sat earlier, and leans his rifle against the wall of the hotel. The sexton helps him into his cassock. Darkness.

PASTOR   Come in, Ill, come into the vestry.

Ill comes in from the left.

PASTOR (*cont.*)   It's dark here, but cool.

ILL   I hope I'm not disturbing you, Pastor.

PASTOR   The House of God is open to all. (*He perceives that Ill's glance has fallen on the rifle.*)   Don't be surprised by the weapon. Mrs. Zachanassian's black panther is prowling about. It was up in the rafters a moment ago, then in the woods of Konradsweil and now in Petersen's barn.

56

ILL   I need protection.

PASTOR   From what?

ILL   I'm afraid.

PASTOR   Afraid? Of whom?

ILL   Of people.

PASTOR   Afraid that people will kill you, Ill?

ILL   They're hunting me like a wild beast.

PASTOR   We should not fear people, but God, not the death of the body, but of the soul. Button the back of my cassock, sexton.

Alongside the walls of the stage, the citizens of Güllen begin to emerge, first the Policeman, then the Mayor, the Four Men, the Painter, and the Teacher, moving stealthily with a vigilant air, rifles at the ready.

ILL   My life is at stake.

PASTOR   Your eternal life.

ILL   Affluence is on the rise.

PASTOR   The ghost of your conscience.

ILL   The people are cheerful. The girls are putting on makeup. The boys are wearing colorful shirts. The town is preparing the feast of my murder, and I am dying of horror.

PASTOR   It's all positive, only positive, what you're going through.

ILL   It's hell.

PASTOR   Hell is within you. You are older than I and you think you know people, but one only knows oneself.

57

Because you once betrayed a girl for money, many years ago, you now think the people, too, will betray you for money. You judge others by your own actions. It's only natural. The source of our anxiety is in our hearts, in our sin. Once you have recognized this, you will be able to conquer what is tormenting you, and you will receive weapons to assist you.

ILL   The Siemethofers bought a washing machine.

PASTOR   Don't worry about that.

ILL   On credit.

PASTOR   You should worry about the immortality of your soul.

ILL   And the Stockers a TV set.

PASTOR   Pray. Sexton, my bands.

The sexton ties the Pastor's bands.

PASTOR (*cont.*)   Search your conscience. Go the way of repentance, otherwise the world will rekindle your fear again and again. It is the only way. We cannot do otherwise.

Silence. The men with their guns disappear. Shadows on the edges of the stage. The fire bell starts clanging.

PASTOR (*cont.*)   Now I must discharge my office, Ill, I have a baptism to perform. The Bible, Sexton, the Liturgy, the Psalter. The baby is starting to scream, it must be moved into safety, into the only glimmer of light that illumines our world.

A second bell begins to ring.

ILL   A second bell?

58

PASTOR   The sound is excellent. Don't you think? Strong and full. Positive, only positive.

ILL (*cries out*)   You, too, Father, you, too!

PASTOR (*throws himself at Ill and holds him tightly*)   Flee! We are weak, Christians and heathen alike. Flee, the bell is resounding in Güllen, the bell of treachery. Flee, and lead us not into temptation by staying.

Two shots are fired. Ill sinks to the ground, Pastor crouches down beside him.

PASTOR (*cont.*)   Flee! Flee!

Ill rises, takes the Pastor's rifle, and exits left.

CLAIRE ZACHANASSIAN   Boby, they're shooting.

BUTLER   Indeed they are, Madam.

CLAIRE ZACHANASSIAN   But why?

BUTLER   The panther escaped.

CLAIRE ZACHANASSIAN   Did they hit him?

BUTLER   He's dead, Madam. Stretched out in front of Ill's shop.

CLAIRE ZACHANASSIAN   Poor little thing. A funeral march, Roby.

Guitar plays a funeral march.

BUTLER   The Gülleners are assembling, Madam, to bring you their condolences.

CLAIRE ZACHANASSIAN   Let them.

The Butler leaves. The Teacher enters from the right with the mixed choir.

TEACHER   Dear Madam.

CLAIRE ZACHANASSIAN   What do you want, teacher of Güllen?

TEACHER   We have been rescued from a great danger. The black panther was balefully prowling our streets. But even though we breathe a sigh of relief, we still deplore the death of such a precious zoological rarity. Wherever human beings settle, the animal world is impoverished. We are not unmindful of this tragic dilemma. We therefore wish to intone a song of choral lamentation. A dirge, Madam, composed by Heinrich Schütz.

CLAIRE ZACHANASSIAN   Very well, let's hear the dirge.

The Teacher begins to conduct. Ill enters from the right with a rifle.

ILL   Quiet!

Frightened, the Gülleners fall silent.

ILL (*cont.*)   This dirge! Why are you singing this dirge!

TEACHER   But Mr. Ill, in view of the black panther's death—

ILL   It's for my death you're practicing this song, for my death!

MAYOR   Now really, Mr. Ill, this is going too far.

ILL   Get out of here! Beat it! Go home!

The Gülleners leave.

CLAIRE ZACHANASSIAN   Take a little spin in your Porsche, Hoby.

HUSBAND VIII   But Hopsi—

CLAIRE ZACHANASSIAN   Scram!

Husband off.

ILL Clara!

CLAIRE ZACHANASSIAN Alfred! Why are you bothering those poor people?

ILL I'm afraid, Clara.

CLAIRE ZACHANASSIAN But it's nice of you. I don't care for this constant singing. I hated it even back in school. Do you remember, Alfred, how we used to run to the woods of Konradsweil when the mixed choir was practicing in front of town hall with the brass band?

ILL Clara. Tell me it's just a show you're putting on, that it's not true, what you're asking for. Say it!

CLAIRE ZACHANASSIAN How strange, Alfred. These memories. I was on a balcony then too, the day we first set eyes on each other. It was an autumn evening like now, no movement in the air, just once in a while a rustling in the trees in the park, and hot. I suppose it's hot now too, though recently I've been freezing all the time. And you were standing there, looking up at me, on and on. I was embarrassed and didn't know what to do. I wanted to go inside, into the dark room, and I couldn't.

ILL I am desperate. I am capable of anything. I warn you, Clara. I am determined to do whatever it takes if you don't tell me now that it's just a joke, a cruel joke. (*He points the gun at her.*)

CLAIRE ZACHANASSIAN And you didn't walk away, down there on the street. You kept staring up at me, looking almost sinister, almost evil, as if you wanted to hurt me, and yet your eyes were full of love.

61

Ill lowers the rifle.

CLAIRE ZACHANASSIAN (*cont.*)   And two fellows were standing next to you, Koby and Loby. They grinned when they saw you staring up at me. And then I left the balcony and went down to where you were. You didn't greet me, didn't say a word to me, but you took my hand, and so we walked away from the town, into the fields, and behind us, like two dogs, Koby and Loby. And then you picked up some stones and threw them at them, and they ran back to the town howling, and we were alone.

The Butler enters from the front right.

CLAIRE ZACHANASSIAN (*cont.*)   Escort me to my room, Boby. I have to dictate some letters to you. After all, I have to transfer a billion from my account.

The Butler escorts her to the room. Koby and Loby come skipping in from up stage.

THE PAIR   The black panther's dead, the black panther's dead.

The balcony disappears. The bell clangs. The stage is set as at the opening of Act One. The station. The only change is a new, untorn timetable on the wall, and somewhere a large poster with a radiant yellow sun: Travel South. Another poster with the legend: Visit the Passion Play in Oberammergau. Also, amid the buildings in the background, a few cranes and some new rooftops. The thunderous, pounding noise of an express train rushing past. The Stationmaster salutes in front of the station. Ill comes from upstage holding a little old suitcase, and looks around. Slowly, as if by chance, citizens of Güllen approach him from all sides. Ill hesitates, stops.

MAYOR   Good morning, Ill.

ALL   Good morning!

ILL (*hesitantly*)   Good morning.

TEACHER   Where are you going with that suitcase?

ALL   Where are you going?

ILL   To the station.

MAYOR   We'll come along!

FIRST MAN   We'll come along!

SECOND MAN   We'll come along!

More and more Gülleners appear.

ILL   There's no need, really. It's not worth the trouble.

MAYOR   Are you going on a trip, Ill?

ILL   I'm going on a trip.

POLICEMAN   And where are you going?

ILL   I don't know. To Kalberstadt, and then on—

TEACHER   Aha—and then on . . .

ILL   To Australia, if possible. I'll find the money somehow. (*Walks on toward the station.*)

THIRD MAN   To Australia!

FOURTH MAN   To Australia!

PAINTER   But why?

ILL (*uncomfortably*)   You can't always stay in the same place— year after year.

He starts running, reaches the station. The others follow at a leisurely pace, surround him.

MAYOR   Emigrating to Australia? That's ridiculous.

DOCTOR   And for you the most dangerous thing to do.

TEACHER   One of those two little eunuchs emigrated to Australia.

POLICEMAN   Right here is where you're most safe.

ALL   Most safe, most safe.

Ill peers about fearfully like a cornered animal.

ILL (*softly*)   I wrote to the governor in Kaffigen.

MAYOR   And?

ILL   No answer.

TEACHER   We can't understand why you're so suspicious.

DOCTOR   No one is trying to kill you.

ALL   No one, no one.

ILL   The post office didn't send the letter.

PAINTER   Impossible.

MAYOR   The postmaster is a member of the town council.

TEACHER   A man of honor.

FIRST MAN   A man of honor!

SECOND MAN   A man of honor!

ILL   Here. A poster: Travel South.

DOCTOR   So what?

ILL   Visit the Passion Play at Oberammergau.

TEACHER   So what?

ILL   There's construction work going on!

MAYOR   So what?

ILL   You're getting richer, more and more affluent!

ALL   So what?

Bell rings.

TEACHER   You see how popular you are.

MAYOR   The whole town's coming along with you.

THIRD MAN   The whole town!

FOURTH MAN   The whole town!

ILL   I didn't ask you to come.

SECOND MAN   Surely we can say good-bye to you.

MAYOR   As old friends.

ALL   As old friends! As old friends!

Noise of a train. The Stationmaster raises his baton. Conductor enters from the left, looking as if he has just jumped off a train.

CONDUCTOR (*with a long-drawn cry*)   Güllen!

MAYOR   That's your train.

ALL   Your train! Your train!

MAYOR   Well, Ill, have a good trip.

ALL   A good trip, a good trip!

DOCTOR   A healthy, happy life!

ALL   A healthy, happy life!

The Gülleners crowd around Ill.

MAYOR It's time. Get on the train to Kalberstadt, and God be with you.

POLICEMAN And lots of luck in Australia!

ALL Lots of luck, lots of luck!

Ill stands motionless, staring at his fellow citizens.

ILL (*softly*) Why are you all here?

POLICEMAN What more do you want?

STATIONMASTER All aboard!

ILL Why are you crowding around me?

MAYOR We're not crowding around you.

ILL Let me pass.

TEACHER But we are letting you pass.

ALL We're letting you pass, we're letting you pass!

ILL One of you will hold me back.

POLICEMAN Nonsense. You just have to get on the train and you'll see it's nonsense.

ILL Go away!

No one moves. Several stand with their hands in their pockets.

MAYOR I don't know what you want. It's up to you to leave. Now get on the train.

ILL Go away!

TEACHER Your fear is simply ridiculous.

Ill falls on his knees.

ILL Why are you standing so close to me!

66

DOCTOR The man has lost his mind.

ILL You want to hold me back.

MAYOR Go ahead! Just get on the train!

ALL Get on the train! Get on the train!

Silence.

ILL (*softly*) One of you will hold me back if I get on the train.

ALL (*insistently*) Nobody! Nobody!

ILL I know it.

POLICEMAN Time is pressing.

TEACHER My dear fellow, will you please get on the train.

ILL I know it! One of you will hold me back! One of you will hold me back!

STATIONMASTER Stand clear!

He raises his baton. The Conductor performs the motions of jumping onto the train. Ill, surrounded by the citizens of Güllen, breaks down and covers his face with his hands.

POLICEMAN You see, you missed it! Now it's rumbling away from you!

Leaving Ill in his state of collapse, all walk slowly toward the back of the stage and disappear.

ILL It's all over!

ACT THREE

Petersen's barn. Claire Zachanassian seated in her sedan chair on the left, motionless, in a white wedding gown, veil, and so on. On the far left, a ladder; also a hay wagon, an old hansom, straw, in the center a small barrel. Rags and moldering sacks hanging from above, enormous spiderwebs spreading in all directions. The Butler comes in from the back.

BUTLER The doctor and the teacher.

CLAIRE ZACHANASSIAN Let them in.

The Doctor and the Teacher appear, groping their way through the dark, finally discover the billionairess, and bow. Both are now dressed in decent, respectable, almost elegant middle-class outfits.

DOCTOR AND TEACHER Madam.

CLAIRE ZACHANASSIAN (*inspecting the two men through her lorgnette*) You look dusty, gentlemen.

The two men wipe dust off their clothes.

TEACHER Excuse us. We had to climb over an old carriage.

CLAIRE ZACHANASSIAN I've retired to Petersen's barn. I need peace and quiet. The wedding in Güllen Cathedral was a strain. After all, I'm not a young girl any more. Sit down on that barrel.

TEACHER Thank you.

He sits down. The Doctor remains standing.

CLAIRE ZACHANASSIAN It's stuffy here. Suffocating. But I love this barn, the smell of hay, straw, and axle grease.

68

Memories. All those tools, the pitchfork, the hansom, the broken hay wagon. They were already here when I was a girl.

TEACHER   A contemplative spot. (*He mops his brow.*)

CLAIRE ZACHANASSIAN   Quite an uplifting sermon the pastor gave.

TEACHER   First Corinthians, thirteen.

CLAIRE ZACHANASSIAN   And you did a decent job too, Teacher, you and your mixed choir. It had a solemn sound.

TEACHER   Bach. From the St. Matthew's Passion. I'm still utterly dazed. Everyone was there, the world of high society, the world of high finance, the world of glamour . . .

CLAIRE ZACHANASSIAN   The worlds have whizzed back to the capital in their Cadillacs. For the wedding feast.

TEACHER   Madam. We don't wish to take up more of your precious time than necessary. Your husband must be waiting for you.

CLAIRE ZACHANASSIAN   Hoby? I sent him back to Geiselgasteig in his Porsche.

DOCTOR   (*bewildered*)   To Geiselgasteig?

CLAIRE ZACHANASSIAN   My lawyers have already filed for divorce.

TEACHER   But Madam, what about the wedding guests?

CLAIRE ZACHANASSIAN   They're used to it. It's my second-shortest marriage. Only the one with Lord Ishmael was even speedier. What brings you here?

TEACHER   We're here in the matter of Mr. Ill.

CLAIRE ZACHANASSIAN Oh, has he died?

TEACHER Madam! We stand by our Western principles.

CLAIRE ZACHANASSIAN So what do you want?

TEACHER The Gülleners have most, most regrettably made a number of acquisitions.

DOCTOR A considerable number.

Both men mop their brows.

CLAIRE ZACHANASSIAN In debt?

TEACHER Hopelessly.

CLAIRE ZACHANASSIAN Despite your principles?

TEACHER We're only human.

DOCTOR And must now pay off our debts.

CLAIRE ZACHANASSIAN You know what has to be done.

TEACHER (*courageously*) Mrs. Zachanassian. Let us speak frankly. Put yourself in our deplorable situation. For two decades I have been planting the tender shoots of humanism in this poverty-stricken community, while our doctor has trundled about in his old Mercedes curing people of rickets and tuberculosis. Such grievous sacrifices. For what? Money? Hardly. Our earnings are minimal, I flatly rejected an offer to teach at Kalberstadt College, and our doctor turned down an appointment at Erlangen University. Pure altruism? That, too, would be saying too much. No, we kept going, all those endless years, and so did this whole little township, because there is a hope, the hope that the bygone greatness of Güllen will be resurrected, that the latent wealth stored in such lavish abundance beneath our native soil will be remembered some day. There is oil

70

beneath Pückenried Valley, and ore beneath the woods of Konradsweil. We are not poor, Madam, we are merely forgotten. We need credit, trust, contracts, and our economy, our culture will flourish. Güllen has something to offer: The Hopewell Foundry.

DOCTOR Bockmann & Co.

TEACHER The Wagner Works. Buy them, modernize them, and Güllen will prosper. Why not invest a hundred million, with a likelihood of high returns, instead of squandering a billion?

CLAIRE ZACHANASSIAN I still have two more.

TEACHER Don't leave us with the knowledge of having waited our whole lives in vain. We are not begging for alms, we're making a business proposition.

CLAIRE ZACHANASSIAN Really. Sounds like a good deal.

TEACHER Madam! I knew you wouldn't let us down.

CLAIRE ZACHANASSIAN Except it's not feasible. I can't buy the Hopewell Foundry, because it's mine already.

TEACHER Yours?

DOCTOR And Bockmann?

TEACHER The Wagner Works?

CLAIRE ZACHANASSIAN I own those too. The factories, Pückenried Valley, Petersen's barn, the town, street by street, house by house. I had my agents buy the whole mess and shut every business down. Your hope was a delusion, your perseverance was pointless, your sacrifices were stupid, and your whole life has been a useless waste.

Silence.

71

DOCTOR   But this is monstrous.

CLAIRE ZACHANASSIAN   It was winter, back then, when I left this town, in a schoolgirl's sailor suit, with red braids, highly pregnant, the townspeople grinning as I passed. Freezing, I sat in the train to Hamburg, but as the outlines of Petersen's barn faded away behind the frosted windowpanes, I decided I would come back one day. Now I am here. Now *I* set the conditions, *I* drive the bargain. (*Loudly.*)   Roby and Toby, to the Golden Apostle. Husband number nine's on the way with his books and manuscripts.

The two brutes emerge from the background and lift the sedan chair.

TEACHER   Mrs. Zachanassian! You are an injured, loving woman. You demand absolute justice. You remind me of a heroine from antiquity, of Medea. But because we understand you in the depths of your soul, you give us the courage to ask more of you: put away these disastrous thoughts of revenge, don't push us to the limit, help these poor, weak, but fundamentally decent people lead a slightly more dignified life, find it in your heart to let human kindness prevail!

CLAIRE ZACHANASSIAN   Human kindness, gentlemen, is made for the purses of millionaires. With financial power like mine, you can afford yourself a new world order. The world made a whore of me, now I'll make a whorehouse of the world. Pay up or get off the dance floor. You want to join the dance? Only paying customers merit respect. And believe me, I'll pay. Güllen for a murder, boom times for a corpse. Get moving, you two!

She is carried off upstage.

DOCTOR   My God, what shall we do?

TEACHER What our conscience demands, Doctor Nüsslin.

Ill's shop appears in the foreground, right. New sign. New gleaming counter, new cash register, costlier merchandise. Whenever someone steps through the imaginary door, a bell rings extravagantly. Behind the counter, Mrs. Ill. First Man enters, left, as a prosperous butcher, a few bloodstains on his new apron.

FIRST MAN What a ceremony. The whole town was out on Cathedral Square watching.

MRS. ILL Clairie deserves some happiness after all that misery.

FIRST MAN Film stars as bridesmaids. With breasts like this.

MRS. ILL They're in fashion these days.

FIRST MAN Cigarettes.

MRS. ILL The green ones?

FIRST MAN Camels. And an ax.

MRS. ILL A butcher's ax?

FIRST MAN Precisely.

MRS. ILL There you are, Mr. Hofbauer.

FIRST MAN Nice merchandise.

MRS. ILL How's business?

FIRST MAN Got new staff.

MRS. ILL I'm hiring too, on the first.

First Man takes the ax. Second Man enters as a well-groomed businessman.

MRS. ILL Hello, Mr. Helmesberger.

Miss Louise walks across the stage in elegant clothing.

FIRST MAN She must be living in a dream, the way she dresses.

MRS. ILL Shameless.

FIRST MAN Aspirin. Went to a party at Stocker's last night.

Mrs. Ill hands First Man the pills with a glass of water.

FIRST MAN Journalists everywhere.

SECOND MAN Snooping around all over town.

FIRST MAN They'll come here too.

MRS. ILL We are ordinary people, Mr. Hofbauer. They won't come looking here.

SECOND MAN They question everyone.

FIRST MAN They're interviewing the pastor right now.

SECOND MAN He'll keep his mouth shut, he's always had a heart for us poor people. Chesterfield.

MRS. ILL On credit?

FIRST MAN On credit. Your husband, Mrs. Ill? Haven't seen him for a long time.

MRS. ILL Upstairs. Pacing the floor. For days now.

FIRST MAN It's his conscience. That was a nasty trick he played on poor Mrs. Zachanassian.

MRS. ILL It hurts me too.

SECOND MAN Ruining the life of a young girl. Bastard. (*firmly*) Mrs. Ill, I hope your husband doesn't blabber when the journalists come.

74

MRS. ILL   Certainly not.

FIRST MAN   Considering his character.

MRS. ILL   It's not easy for me, Mr. Hofbauer.

FIRST MAN   If he tries to expose Clara by claiming she put a price on his head or something like that, when actually it was just an expression of unspeakable suffering, we'll just have to take action.

SECOND MAN   Not because of the billion.

FIRST MAN   As an expression of public indignation. Poor Mrs. Zachanassian has been through more than enough on account of him. (*He looks around.*)   Is this the way up to the apartment?

MRS. ILL   It's the only way up. Inconvenient. But we're renovating in the spring.

FIRST MAN   I might as well plant myself here.

First Man plants himself on the far right, arms folded, with his ax, like a guard. The Teacher enters.

MRS. ILL   Why, here's our good teacher. How nice of you to come and see us.

TEACHER   I need a strong alcoholic beverage.

MRS. ILL   Steinhäger?

TEACHER   A shot.

MRS. ILL   You too, Mr. Hofbauer?

FIRST MAN   No thanks. Still have to drive my Volkswagen to Kaffigen. To buy some piglets.

MRS. ILL   And you, Mr. Helmesberger?

SECOND MAN   I won't have a drop till these damned journalists have left town.

Mrs. Ill fills a shot glass for the Teacher.

TEACHER   Thanks. (*Downs his drink with one gulp.*)

MRS. ILL   You're trembling, sir.

TEACHER   I've been drinking too much lately. Just come from the Golden Apostle, they're having a regular alcohol orgy there. I hope you don't mind my breath.

MRS. ILL   One more won't do any harm. (*Pours him another one.*)

TEACHER   Your husband?

MRS. ILL   Upstairs. Constantly pacing.

TEACHER   Another glass. The last one. (*Pours it himself.*)

The Painter enters left. New corduroy suit, gaily colored neckerchief, black beret.

PAINTER   Watch out. Two journalists asked me about this store.

FIRST MAN   Suspicious.

PAINTER   I pretended not to know anything.

SECOND MAN   Smart.

PAINTER   Hope they come to my studio. I'm painting a Christ figure.

The Teacher pours himself another drink. Outside, the two women from Act Two walk by, smartly dressed, and look at the merchandise in the imaginary shopwindow.

FIRST MAN   Those women.

76

SECOND MAN Going to the new movie theater in broad daylight.

Third Man enters left.

THIRD MAN The press.

SECOND MAN Keep your mouth shut.

PAINTER Make sure he doesn't come down.

FIRST MAN That will be taken care of.

The Gülleners assemble on the right. The Teacher has half emptied the bottle and remains standing by the counter. Two Journalists enter with cameras. The Fourth Man appears behind them.

JOURNALIST I Good evening, folks.

GÜLLENERS Good evening.

JOURNALIST I Question number one: How do you all feel, generally speaking?

FIRST MAN (*uneasily*) We're pleased, of course, about Mrs. Zachanassian's visit.

THIRD MAN Pleased.

PAINTER Moved.

SECOND MAN Proud.

JOURNALIST I Proud.

FOURTH MAN After all, Clairie's one of us.

JOURNALIST I Question number two is for the lady behind the counter: some people claim that your husband preferred you to Mrs. Zachanassian.

Silence.

77

FIRST MAN Who made that claim?

JOURNALIST I Those two fat little blind men that came with Mrs. Zachanassian.

Silence.

FOURTH MAN (*hesitantly*) What did the little men tell you?

JOURNALIST II Everything.

PAINTER Damn.

Silence.

JOURNALIST II Claire Zachanassian and the owner of this store were on the verge of getting married more than forty years ago. True?

Silence.

MRS. ILL True.

JOURNALIST II Mr. Ill?

MRS. ILL In Kalberstadt.

ALL In Kalberstadt.

JOURNALIST I We can picture the romance. Mr. Ill and Claire Zachanassian growing up together, maybe next door to each other, going to school together, walking in the woods, first kisses, et cetera, until Mr. Ill meets you, Ma'am, as something new and unfamiliar, as passion itself.

MRS. ILL It happened just the way you said.

JOURNALIST I Claire Zachanassian gets the picture, bows out in her quiet, noble way, and you marry—

MRS. ILL For love.

78

THE OTHER GÜLLENERS (*relieved*)   For love.

JOURNALIST I   For love.

With an air of indifference, the two newspapermen write in their notepads. Roby enters from the right, leading the two eunuchs by their ears.

THE PAIR (*wailing*)   We won't tell any more stories, we won't tell any more stories.

They are led upstage, where Toby awaits them with a whip.

THE PAIR (*cont.*)   Not to Toby, not to Toby!

JOURNALIST II   Your husband, Mrs. Ill, doesn't he now and then, I mean, it would only be human if, now and then, he had some regrets.

MRS. ILL   Money alone makes no one happy.

JOURNALIST II   No one happy.

Enter Son, left, wearing a buckskin jacket.

MRS. ILL   Our son, Karl.

JOURNALIST I   Splendid young man.

JOURNALIST II   Does he know about the relations . . .

MRS. ILL   We have no secrets in our family. My husband always says: whatever God knows, our children should know too.

JOURNALIST I   God knows.

JOURNALIST II   Children should know.

The Daughter walks into the store, wearing a tennis outfit, holding a tennis racket.

MRS. ILL   Our daughter, Ottilie.

JOURNALIST II   Charming.

The Teacher now rouses himself to action.

TEACHER   Gülleners. I am your old teacher. I have been drinking my Steinhäger and kept my thoughts to myself. But now I want to hold a speech, about the old lady's visit to Güllen. (*He climbs onto the small barrel, left from the scene in Petersen's barn.*)

FIRST MAN   Have you lost your mind?

SECOND MAN   Cut it out.

THIRD MAN   Get off that barrel!

TEACHER   Gülleners! I want to proclaim the truth, even if our poverty should last forever!

MRS. ILL   You are drunk, sir. You should be ashamed of yourself.

TEACHER   Ashamed? You should be ashamed, woman, for you are about to betray your husband!

SON   Shut up!

FOURTH MAN   Get out!

TEACHER   Calamity is battening, beware! As in Oedipus: swollen like a toad!

DAUGHTER (*supplicating*)   Please, sir!

TEACHER   Child, you disappoint me. It's you who ought to be speaking out, and now your old teacher must do so, with a voice of thunder!

PAINTER (*dragging him off the barrel*)   Are you trying to wreck my chances as an artist? I just finished painting a Christ, a Christ!

TEACHER   I protest! I appeal to world opinion! Something monstrous is in the making here in Güllen!

The Gülleners fall upon him, but at this moment Ill enters, right, wearing ragged old clothes.

ILL   What's going on in my store!

The Gülleners let go of the Teacher and stare at Ill, frightened. Deathly silence.

TEACHER   The truth, Ill. I'm telling the gentlemen of the press the truth. I'm telling it like an archangel, with a ringing voice. (*He sways.*)   For I am a humanist, a friend of the ancient Greeks, an admirer of Plato.

ILL   Be quiet.

TEACHER   But humanity—

ILL   Sit down.

Silence.

TEACHER (*sobered*)   Sit down. Humanity has to sit down. Absolutely—if even you won't stand up for the truth. (*He sits down on the barrel, trying to find his balance.*)

ILL (*to the journalists*)   I'm sorry about this. The man is drunk.

JOURNALIST I   Mr. Ill?

ILL   What do you want of me?

JOURNALIST I   We're very pleased to meet you after all. We need some pictures. May we? (*He looks around.*)   Groceries, household items, hardware—I have an idea: sell the ax.

ILL The ax?

JOURNALIST I To the butcher. He already has it in his hand. Hand me that murder weapon for a moment, my friend. (*He takes the ax from First Man's hand. Demonstrates.*) You take the ax, weigh it in your hand, make a thoughtful face, you see, like that; and you, Mr. Ill, lean across the counter, advising the butcher. (*He arranges the two men in their positions.*) More natural, gentlemen, more casual.

The reporters take their photographs.

JOURNALIST I (*cont.*) That was good, really good.

JOURNALIST II May I ask you now to put your arm around your wife's shoulders. The son on the left, the daughter on the right. And now I want to see you beaming with happiness, beaming, beaming, from deep inside, just beaming with cheerful, quiet contentment.

JOURNALIST I That's what I call beaming.

JOURNALIST II Finished.

Several photographers come running in downstage left, cross the length of the stage, and exit upstage right. One of them shouts into the store.

PHOTOGRAPHER Zachanassian's got a new one. They're taking a walk in the woods of Konradsweil.

JOURNALIST I A new one!

JOURNALIST II That's good for a *Life* magazine cover.

The two newspaper reporters run out of the store. Silence. The First Man is still holding the ax in his hand.

FIRST MAN (*relieved*) That was lucky.

PAINTER (*to the Teacher*) With all due respect, sir, if we still want to settle this business amicably, the press has to be kept out of it. Got it?

He exits. Second Man follows him, but pauses in front of Ill before exiting.

SECOND MAN Smart. Very smart of you to keep your mouth shut.

THIRD MAN No one would believe a bastard like you anyway. (*He exits. Fourth Man spits and exits.*)

FIRST MAN We'll be in the picture magazines now, Ill.

ILL Right.

FIRST MAN We'll be famous.

ILL Sort of.

FIRST MAN A Corona.

ILL Sure.

FIRST MAN Charge it.

ILL Of course.

FIRST MAN Frankly, only a son of a bitch would do what you did to Clairie.

He is about to leave.

ILL The ax, Hofbauer.

First Man hesitates, returns the ax to Ill, and exits. Silence in the store. The Teacher is still sitting on his barrel.

TEACHER I apologize. I had a few nips of Steinhäger, two or three.

ILL That's all right.

The family cross to the right and exit.

TEACHER I wanted to help you. But they beat me down, and you didn't want it either. Oh, Ill. What sort of people are we? That disgraceful billion is burning in our hearts. Pull yourself together, fight for your life, get in touch with the press. You're running out of time.

ILL I'm not fighting any more.

TEACHER (*astounded*) Tell me, are you so scared that you've completely lost your mind?

ILL I realized I have no right any more.

TEACHER No right? Compared to this damned old lady, this shameless archwhore, switching husbands in front of our eyes, collecting our souls?

ILL After all, it's my fault.

TEACHER Your fault?

ILL I turned Clara into what she is, and myself into what I am, a grimy, petty shopkeeper. What shall I do, teacher of Güllen? Play the innocent? It's all my own doing, the eunuchs, the butler, the coffin, and the billion. I can't help myself anymore, and I can't help you either.

The Teacher stands up with an effort, swaying only slightly.

TEACHER I'm sober. Suddenly. (*Walks over to Ill, swaying.*) You are right. Absolutely. It's all your fault. And now I want to tell you something, Alfred Ill, something fundamental. (*He stands facing Ill, rigidly upright, swaying only a little.*) They will kill you. I've known it from the beginning, and you too have known it for a long time, even

84

though no one else in Güllen wants to admit it. The temptation is too great and our poverty is too wretched. But I know something else. I too will take part in it. I can feel myself slowly turning into a murderer. My faith in humanity is powerless. And because I know this, I have turned into a drunk. I am scared, Ill, just as you have been scared. I still know that some day an old lady will visit us too, and that then what is happening to you now will happen to us, but soon, maybe in a few hours, I will no longer know it. (*Silence.*)   Another bottle of Steinhäger.

Ill puts a bottle in front of him. The Teacher hesitates, then makes up his mind and takes the bottle.

TEACHER (*cont.*)   Put it on my account. (*He walks out slowly.*)

The family return. Ill looks around the store as if dreaming.

ILL   Everything's new. Modern, the way our place looks now. Clean, attractive. I've always dreamed of having a store like this. (*He takes the tennis racket from his daughter's hand.*)   You play tennis?

DAUGHTER   I've had a couple of lessons.

ILL   Early in the morning, right? Instead of going to the Employment Office?

DAUGHTER   All my friends play tennis.

Silence.

ILL   I was looking out the window, Karl. I saw you in an automobile.

SON   It's just an Opel Olympia, they're not that expensive.

ILL   When did you learn to drive?

Silence.

85

ILL (*cont.*) Instead of looking for work in the blazing sun?

SON Sometimes. (*Embarrassed, the Son picks up the small barrel on which the Teacher was sitting and carries it off the stage, right.*)

ILL I was looking for my Sunday suit. I found a fur coat next to it.

MRS. ILL It's on approval.

Silence.

MRS. ILL (*cont.*) Everyone's running up debts, Freddy. You're the only one who goes into a panic about it. It's simply ridiculous for you to be scared. It's so obvious this thing will be settled peacefully, without anyone touching a hair on your head. Clairie won't go through with it; I know her, she's too good-hearted.

DAUGHTER Definitely, father.

SON It makes sense. Don't you see?

Silence.

ILL (*slowly*) It's Saturday. Son, I'd like to go for a drive in your car, just once. In *our* car.

SON (*uncertainly*) You want to?

ILL All of you, put on your good clothes. We'll go for a drive together.

MRS. ILL (*uncertainly*) You want me to come too? That wouldn't look right.

ILL Why shouldn't it look right? Put on your fur coat. You've never worn it before: this is a good occasion. I'll make up the accounts in the meantime.

86

Exit Mother and Daughter, right, and Son, left, while Ill is busy at the cash register. Enter Mayor, left, with the rifle.

MAYOR   Good evening, Ill. Don't let me disturb you. I'm just passing by.

ILL   By all means.

Silence.

MAYOR   I brought you a gun.

ILL   Thanks.

MAYOR   It's loaded.

ILL   I don't need it.

The Mayor leans the rifle against the counter.

MAYOR   Tonight there's a community meeting. At the Golden Apostle. In the auditorium.

ILL   I'll be there.

MAYOR   Everyone will be there. We'll discuss your case. We're sort of in a bind.

ILL   That's my impression too.

MAYOR   The motion will be rejected.

ILL   Possibly.

MAYOR   You can never be sure, of course.

ILL   Of course.

Silence.

MAYOR (*cautiously*)   In such a case, would you accept the judgment, Ill? Since the press will be there.

87

ILL   The press?

MAYOR   The radio too, and the TV, and the weekly newsreels. A touchy situation, not just for you but for us as well, believe me. As the lady's hometown, and especially after her wedding in the cathedral, we've become so famous that they're preparing a program about our ancient democratic institutions.

ILL (*busying himself with the cash register*)   You're not going to make the lady's offer known to the public?

MAYOR   Not directly—only the insiders will understand the meaning of the discussion.

ILL   The fact that my life is at stake.

Silence.

MAYOR   I am advising the press to the effect that Mrs. Zachanassian may—possibly—set up an endowment, which you, Ill, helped bring about, thanks to your early friendship with her. That you were friends is of course common knowledge now. This means that as far as appearances go, you're clear of all guilt, no matter what happens.

ILL   That's kind of you.

MAYOR   Frankly, I didn't do it for you but for your perfectly decent, honest family.

ILL   I understand.

MAYOR   You have to admit we're playing fair with you. Up till now you've kept quiet. Good. But will you continue to be quiet? If you intend to talk, we'll have to do the whole thing without a community meeting.

ILL   I get the point.

MAYOR Well?

ILL I'm glad to hear an open threat.

MAYOR I'm not threatening you, Ill, you're threatening us. If you talk, we'll have to act. In advance.

ILL I'll keep quiet.

MAYOR No matter what tonight's decision will be?

ILL I'll accept it.

MAYOR Fine.

Silence.

MAYOR (*cont.*) I'm glad you'll submit to the community's judgment, Ill. There's still a glimmer of decency in you. But wouldn't it be better if we didn't even have to have a community meeting to judge your case?

ILL What are you trying to say?

MAYOR You said before that you didn't need the rifle. Perhaps now you need it after all.

Silence.

MAYOR (*cont.*) Then we could tell the lady that we had brought you to justice and still receive the money. I've spent many a sleepless night over this proposal, believe me. But wouldn't it be your duty, as a man of honor, to face the facts and put an end to your life? If only for the sake of the community, out of love for your hometown. You're well aware of our wretched poverty, the misery, the hungry children . . .

ILL You're all doing quite well now.

MAYOR Ill!

89

ILL   Your Honor! I've been through hell. I saw you all going into debt, and with every sign of prosperity I felt death creeping closer. If you had spared me that anguish, that horrible fear, it would have all been different, we could speak on different terms, I would take the rifle. For all of your sake. But then I shut myself in, conquered my fear. Alone. It was hard; now it's done. There is no turning back. Now you must be my judges. I will submit to your decision, whatever it turns out to be. For me it will be justice; I don't know what it will be for you. May God help you live with your judgment. You can kill me, I won't complain, I won't protest, I won't defend myself, but your action is yours, and I can't relieve you of it.

MAYOR (*taking back the rifle*)   Too bad. You're missing a chance to redeem yourself and become a halfway decent human being. But obviously that was too much to expect.

ILL   A light, Your Honor. (*He lights the Mayor's cigarette.*)

Exit Mayor.

Enter Mrs. Ill in a fur coat, the Daughter in a red dress.

ILL (*cont.*)   You look very distinguished, Matilda.

MRS. ILL   Persian lamb.

ILL   Like a lady.

MRS. ILL   Rather expensive.

ILL   Lovely dress, Ottilie. But a little risqué, don't you think?

DAUGHTER   Oh, come on, Daddy. You should see my evening dress.

The store disappears. The Son puts four chairs on the empty stage.

ILL Beautiful car. All my life I tried to put a little money aside, to be able to afford some comfort, something like this car, and now that the time has come I'd like to know what it feels like. Matilda, you get in the back with me, Ottilie, you sit in the front next to Karl.

They sit down on the chairs, miming an automobile ride.

SON I can do eighty miles an hour.

ILL Not so fast. I want to see the scenery, the town I've lived in for almost seventy years. Nice and clean now, the old streets, lots of renovation. Gray smoke above the chimneys, geraniums in front of the windows, sunflowers, roses in the gardens by the Goethe Arch, children laughing, couples everywhere. Nice modern building on Brahms Square.

MRS. ILL They're renovating the Café Hodel.

DAUGHTER The doctor with his Mercedes 300.

ILL The plain, the hills behind it, as if covered with gold today. Tremendous, the shadows we're diving into, and then the light again. The cranes of the Wagner Works like giants on the horizon, and the Bockmann chimneys.

SON The town wants to buy them.

ILL What?

SON The town wants to buy them. (*He toots the horn.*)

MRS. ILL Funny little cars.

SON Messerschmidts. Every apprentice has to have one.

DAUGHTER C'est terrible.

MRS. ILL Ottilie is taking advanced courses in French and English.

ILL   Good idea. Kübler's bar and grill. Haven't been out here for a long time.

SON   It's going to be an eatery.

ILL   You have to talk louder at this speed.

SON (*louder*)   It's going to be an eatery. Stocker, of course. Passing everyone in his Buick.

DAUGHTER   Un nouveau riche.

ILL   Now drive through Pückenried Valley. Past the moor and down Poplar Boulevard, around Prince Hasso's hunting lodge. Enormous clouds piled up in the sky, as if it were summer. Beautiful country, flooded in evening light. I'm seeing it today as if for the first time.

DAUGHTER   It's an atmosphere like in Adalbert Stifter.

ILL   Like where?

MRS. ILL   Ottilie's studying literature too.

ILL   Cultivated.

SON   Hofbauer with his Volkswagen. Coming back from Kaffigen.

DAUGHTER   With the piglets.

MRS. ILL   Karl's a good driver. Elegant, the way he cut that corner. You're in safe hands with him.

SON   First gear. The road's steep here.

ILL   Always got out of breath walking up this hill.

MRS. ILL   Glad I've got my fur coat. It's getting cool.

ILL   You've gone the wrong way. This is the road to Beisenbach. You have to go back and then left, into the woods of Konradsweil.

Enter the four citizens with the wooden bench, wearing tuxedos now, representing trees.

FIRST MAN   Once again we're pines and beeches,

SECOND MAN   Finch and cuckoo, timid deer.

THIRD MAN   Moldering roots and domes of ivy.

FOURTH MAN   Deep primeval forest gloom.

Son toots his horn.

SON   Another deer. The beast won't leave the road.

Third Man leaps away.

DAUGHTER   They're trusting. No one's poaching any more.

ILL   Stop under those trees.

SON   All right.

MRS. ILL   What do you want to do?

ILL   Walk in the woods. (*Stands up.*)   Beautiful, the sound of the bells of Güllen. The workday's over.

SON   Four bells. Now it sounds just right.

ILL   Everything's yellow. Fall is really here. Leaves on the ground like heaps of gold. (*He tramps around in the woods.*)

SON   We'll wait for you down by Güllen Bridge.

ILL   Not necessary. I'll walk to town through the woods. To the community meeting.

93

MRS. ILL In that case we'll drive to Kalberstadt, Freddy, and go to a movie.

DAUGHTER Au revoir, papa.

MRS. ILL See you soon! See you soon!

The family disappear with the chairs. Ill gazes after them. He sits down on the wooden bench, which is on the left.

Soughing sound of wind. Enter Toby and Roby, right, carrying Claire Zachanassian in her sedan chair. She is wearing her familiar clothes. Roby has a guitar slung over his back. HUSBAND IX *is striding beside her, a Nobel Prize winner, tall, slender, salt-and-pepper hair, a moustache. (May be played by the same actor as the earlier husbands.) Behind them the Butler.*

CLAIRE ZACHANASSIAN The woods of Konradsweil, Roby and Toby, stop for a moment.

Claire Zachanassian climbs out of the sedan chair, looks at the forest through her lorgnette, strokes the back of the First Man.

CLAIRE ZACHANASSIAN (*cont.*) Bark beetles. The tree is dying. (*She notices Ill.*) Alfred! Good to see you. I'm visiting my woods.

ILL Are the woods yours too?

CLAIRE ZACHANASSIAN They are. May I sit next to you?

ILL By all means. I just said good-bye to my family. They're going to a movie. Karl bought himself a car.

CLAIRE ZACHANASSIAN Progress. (*She sits down to the right of Ill.*)

ILL Ottilie is taking a literature course. English and French as well.

94

CLAIRE ZACHANASSIAN You see, they've developed a sense of ideals after all. Come, Zoby, make your bow. My ninth husband. Nobel Prize winner.

ILL Pleased to meet you.

CLAIRE ZACHANASSIAN He's especially remarkable when he doesn't think. Stop thinking for a moment, Zoby.

HUSBAND IX But Schatzi . . .

CLAIRE ZACHANASSIAN Oh, don't be coy.

HUSBAND IX All right. (*He stops thinking.*)

CLAIRE ZACHANASSIAN See? Now he looks like a diplomat. Reminds me of Count Holk, though that one didn't write books. He wants to retire so he can write his memoirs and manage my estate.

ILL Congratulations.

CLAIRE ZACHANASSIAN It makes me uneasy. Husbands are objects for display, not for daily use. Zoby, go and do some research. You'll find the historical ruins on the left.

Husband IX goes off to do research. Ill looks around.

ILL The two eunuchs?

CLAIRE ZACHANASSIAN Started talking too much. I had them shipped off to Hong Kong, to one of my opium dens. There they can smoke and dream. The butler will follow them soon. I won't be needing him either. Boby, hand me a Romeo et Juliette.*

Butler emerges from the background, hands her a cigarette case.

---

*A brand of cigarettes.

CLAIRE ZACHANASSIAN (*cont.*)   Would you like one too, Alfred?

ILL   I would, thanks.

CLAIRE ZACHANASSIAN   Help yourself. Give us a light, Boby.

They smoke.

ILL   Smells really good.

CLAIRE ZACHANASSIAN   We often smoked together in these woods. Do you remember? Cigarettes you had bought from little Matilda. Or stolen.

First Man taps a key against his pipe.

CLAIRE ZACHANASSIAN (*cont.*)   That woodpecker again.

FOURTH MAN   Cuckoo! Cuckoo!

ILL   And the cuckoo.

CLAIRE ZACHANASSIAN   Would you like Roby to play for you on his guitar?

ILL   Please.

CLAIRE ZACHANASSIAN   He plays well, the pardoned murderer. I need him for my contemplative moments. I hate record players and radios too.

ILL   "There's a Battalion on the March in Deepest Africa."

CLAIRE ZACHANASSIAN   Your favorite song. I taught it to him.

Silence. They smoke. Cuckoo and so on. Soughing wind. Roby plays the ballad.

ILL   You had—I mean, we had a child?

CLAIRE ZACHANASSIAN We did.

ILL Was it a boy or a girl?

CLAIRE ZACHANASSIAN A girl.

ILL And what name did you give her?

CLAIRE ZACHANASSIAN Geneviève.

ILL Pretty name.

CLAIRE ZACHANASSIAN I only saw the thing once. At birth. Then it was taken away. By the Christian Welfare Society.

ILL Her eyes?

CLAIRE ZACHANASSIAN They weren't open yet.

ILL Hair?

CLAIRE ZACHANASSIAN Black, I believe, but that's not unusual with a newborn.

ILL I guess you're right.

Silence. Smoking. Guitar.

ILL (*cont.*) Where was she when she died?

CLAIRE ZACHANASSIAN With people. I forgot their names.

ILL What did she die of?

CLAIRE ZACHANASSIAN Meningitis. Maybe it was something else. I received a card from the authorities.

ILL In cases of death you can depend on them.

Silence.

CLAIRE ZACHANASSIAN I told you about our little girl. Now you tell me about myself.

97

ILL   About you?

CLAIRE ZACHANASSIAN   What I was like when I was seventeen, when you loved me.

ILL   Once I had to look for you for a long time in Petersen's barn. I found you in the carriage with nothing on but a shift and a long straw between your lips.

CLAIRE ZACHANASSIAN   You were strong and brave. You fought the railroad man when he tried to sneak up on me. I wiped the blood from your face with my red petticoat.

The guitar playing stops.

CLAIRE ZACHANASSIAN (*cont.*)   The ballad is over.

ILL   One more: "Home Sweet Home."

CLAIRE ZACHANASSIAN   Roby can play that too.

Guitar plays again.

ILL   The hour has come. For the last time we're sitting in our evil forest full of cuckoos and sighing winds.

The trees move their branches.

ILL (*cont.*)   The town's holding a meeting this evening. They'll sentence me to death, and one of them will kill me. I don't know who he will be or where it will happen, I only know that I'm ending a meaningless life.

CLAIRE ZACHANASSIAN   I loved you. You betrayed me. But the dream of life, of love, of trust—this dream that was a reality once—I haven't forgotten that. I want to rebuild it with my billions, I will change the past, by destroying you.

ILL   Thank you for the wreaths, the chrysanthemums, and the roses.

98

More soughing wind.

ILL (*cont.*)   They'll look good on the coffin in the Golden Apostle. Distinguished.

CLAIRE ZACHANASSIAN   I will take you to Capri in your coffin. I built a mausoleum in the garden of my palazzo. Surrounded by cypresses. Overlooking the Mediterranean.

ILL   I only know it from pictures.

CLAIRE ZACHANASSIAN   Deep blue. A grand panorama. There you will remain. With me.

ILL   Now "Home Sweet Home" is finished too.

Husband IX returns.

CLAIRE ZACHANASSIAN   The Nobel Prize winner. Back from his ruin. Well, Zoby?

HUSBAND IX   Early Christian. Destroyed by the Huns.

CLAIRE ZACHANASSIAN   Too bad. Your arm. The sedan chair, Roby and Toby.

She climbs into the sedan chair.

CLAIRE ZACHANASSIAN (*cont.*)   Farewell, Alfred.

ILL   Farewell, Clara.

The sedan chair is carried away upstage. Ill remains seated on the bench. The trees put away their branches. A stage portal descends, with the usual curtains and draperies, and an inscription: "Life is serious, art serene." The Policeman emerges from upstage, wearing a splendid new uniform, and sits down next to Ill. A RADIO REPORTER enters, begins talking into the microphone while the Gülleners assemble. Everyone in festive new clothes, the men in tuxedos. Swarms of news photographers, journalists, film cameras.

99

RADIO REPORTER Ladies and gentlemen. Now that we've been at the birthplace and talked with the pastor, we will attend a community meeting. We are nearing the climax of the visit Mrs. Claire Zachanassian is paying to her friendly, cozy little hometown. The famous lady is not personally present, but the mayor will make an important announcement in her name. We are in the auditorium of the Golden Apostle, the very same hotel in which Goethe spent a night. On the stage, which is ordinarily used for club events as well as for guest shows of the Kalberstadt Repertory Theater, the men of Güllen are now assembling, an ancient custom, as the mayor has just informed us. The women are all down in the auditorium—another traditional feature. The atmosphere is solemn, the tension extraordinary, all the weekly newsreels are here, my colleagues from TV, reporters from all over the world, and now the mayor is beginning to speak.

The Reporter, holding his microphone, walks over to the Mayor, who is standing center stage, with the men of Güllen surrounding him in a semicircle.

MAYOR I welcome the community of Güllen. I hereby open this meeting. We have a single item on our agenda. It is my privilege to announce that Mrs. Claire Zachanassian, the daughter of our worthy fellow citizen Gottfried Wäscher, intends to make a donation to us in the amount of one billion.

Murmurs among the Press.

MAYOR (*cont.*) Five hundred million to the city, five hundred million to be shared among all the townspeople.

Silence.

RADIO REPORTER (*with subdued voice*)   Dear listeners, this is a sensational moment. An endowment that turns the inhabitants of this small town into wealthy people overnight. This represents one of the greatest social experiments of our time. Naturally, the community is stunned. There is a deathly silence here. Deep emotion on every face.

MAYOR   I now yield the floor to our teacher.

The Radio Reporter moves closer to the Teacher, still holding out his microphone.

TEACHER   Gülleners. We must be aware of the fact that in making this donation, Mrs. Zachanassian has a definite purpose. What is this purpose? Is it to make us happy, to shower us with gold, to renovate the Wagner Works, the Hopewell Foundry, Bockmann & Co.? You know this is not the case. Mrs. Claire Zachanassian has more important plans. What she wants for her billion is justice. Justice. She wants to see our community transformed into a citadel of justice. This demand bids us pause. Were we not already a just community?

FIRST MAN   Never!

SECOND MAN   We tolerated a crime!

THIRD MAN   A miscarriage of justice!

FOURTH MAN   Perjury!

A WOMAN'S VOICE   A bastard!

OTHER VOICES   That's right!

TEACHER   People of Güllen! This is the sad state of affairs: we tolerated injustice. Now I am fully aware of what a billion would mean to us in terms of material advantages. Nor am I

ignorant of the blight and the bitterness caused by poverty.
And yet: the issue here is not money—(*tremendous
applause*) —it is not prosperity, a comfortable way of life,
luxury; the issue is whether we want to make justice a
reality, and not only justice but all the ideals for which our
ancient forebears lived and struggled and for which they
died, ideals that constitute the true value of our Western
world. (*Tremendous applause.*) Freedom is at stake when a
man violates the tenets of neighborly love, when the com-
mandment to succor the weak is disregarded, when the
institution of marriage is insulted, when a court of justice is
deceived, and a young mother is plunged into misery. (*Boos.*)
Now, in God's name, the time has come for us to act on our
ideals in earnest, indeed in dead earnest. (*Tremendous
applause.*) Abundance has meaning only if it produces an
abundance of grace. But grace comes only to those who
hunger for grace. Do you have this hunger, Gülleners, this
hunger of the spirit, and not just that other hunger, the
hunger of the body, physical and profane? That is the urgent
question that I as principal of your high school have for you.
Only if you are unable to tolerate evil, only if you are
incapable of living any longer, under any circumstances, in a
world of injustice, can you accept Mrs. Zachanassian's billion
and fulfill the conditions that are attached to this endowment.
This, Gülleners, I beg you to consider.

Thunderous applause.

RADIO REPORTER You hear the applause, ladies and
gentlemen. I am overwhelmed. With this speech, the
principal has evinced a moral greatness that is—alas—not
commonly found in our time. Courageously he pointed his
finger at the general run of abuse and injustice that is
encountered in every community, wherever there are
human beings.

MAYOR Alfred Ill—

RADIO REPORTER The mayor is taking the floor again.

MAYOR Alfred Ill, I have a question to ask you.

The Policeman gives Ill a shove. Ill stands up. The Radio Reporter goes to him with the microphone.

RADIO REPORTER Now the voice of the man upon whose suggestion the Zachanassian endowment was founded, the voice of Alfred Ill, the childhood friend of the town's benefactress. Alfred Ill is a sturdy man of about seventy, an upright Güllener of the old school, deeply moved, of course, full of gratitude, full of quiet satisfaction.

MAYOR It is owing to you that the endowment was offered to us, Alfred Ill. Are you aware of this?

Ill says something inaudible.

RADIO REPORTER You must speak louder, dear sir, so that our listeners can hear you.

ILL Yes.

MAYOR Will you respect our decision concerning the acceptance or rejection of the Claire Zachanassian Endowment?

ILL I respect it.

MAYOR Does anyone wish to pose a question to Alfred Ill?

Silence.

MAYOR (*cont.*) Does anyone wish to comment on Mrs. Zachanassian's endowment?

Silence.

MAYOR (*cont.*)   Our pastor?

Silence.

MAYOR (*cont.*)   Our physician?

Silence.

MAYOR (*cont.*)   The police?

Silence.

MAYOR (*cont.*)   The opposition party?

Silence.

MAYOR (*cont.*)   I now call for a vote.

Silence. Only the hum of the film cameras, the flash of the flashbulbs.

MAYOR (*cont.*)   All those who sincerely want justice done, raise your hands.

All except Ill raise their hands.

RADIO REPORTER   Devout silence in the auditorium. Nothing but a single sea of raised hands, like a mighty conspiracy to promote a better, more just world. Only the old man sits motionless, overcome with joy. He has reached his goal, the endowment has become a reality, thanks to the generosity of his childhood friend.

MAYOR   The Claire Zachanassian Endowment has been accepted. Unanimously. Not for the sake of money—

THE COMMUNITY   Not for the sake of money—

MAYOR   But for the sake of justice—

THE COMMUNITY   But for the sake of justice—

MAYOR   And to allay our conscience.

104

THE COMMUNITY And to allay our conscience.

MAYOR For we cannot live if we sanction a crime in our midst—

THE COMMUNITY For we cannot live if we sanction a crime in our midst—

MAYOR Which we must eradicate—

THE COMMUNITY Which we must eradicate—

MAYOR So that our souls do not suffer damage—

THE COMMUNITY So that our souls do not suffer damage—

MAYOR And our most sacred goods.

THE COMMUNITY And our most sacred goods.

ILL (*screams*) My God!

Everyone stands with solemnly raised hands, but now there is a mishap with the newsreel camera.

CAMERAMAN What a pity, Your Honor. Our lights gave out. Let's do that final vote again.

MAYOR Again?

CAMERAMAN For the newsreel.

MAYOR Oh, of course.

CAMERAMAN Lights?

A VOICE Lights.

CAMERAMAN Roll.

The Mayor strikes a pose.

MAYOR All those who from the bottom of their hearts want justice done, raise your hands.

All except Ill raise their hands.

MAYOR The Claire Zachanassian Endowment has been accepted. Unanimously. Not for the sake of the money—

THE COMMUNITY Not for the sake of the money—

MAYOR But for the sake of justice—

THE COMMUNITY But for the sake of justice—

MAYOR And to allay our conscience.

THE COMMUNITY And to allay our conscience.

MAYOR For we cannot live if we sanction a crime in our midst—

THE COMMUNITY For we cannot live if we sanction a crime in our midst—

MAYOR Which we must eradicate—

THE COMMUNITY Which we must eradicate—

MAYOR So that our souls do not suffer damage—

THE COMMUNITY So that our souls do not suffer damage—

MAYOR And our most sacred goods.

THE COMMUNITY And our most sacred goods.

Silence.

CAMERAMAN (*softly*) Ill! Come on!

Silence.

CAMERAMAN (*cont.*) (*disappointed*) Then not. It's a pity that joyful cry, "My God," didn't come, it was particularly impressive.

MAYOR The gentlemen of the press, radio, and cinema are invited to a repast. In the restaurant. The easiest way out of the auditorium is through the stage exit. For the ladies, tea is being served in the garden of the Golden Apostle.

The press, cinema, and radio people exit upstage right. The men of Güllen remain on the stage, immobile. Ill stands up, wants to leave.

POLICEMAN Stay! (*He pushes Ill down to the bench.*)

ILL You're planning to do it today?

POLICEMAN Of course.

ILL I thought it would be best if it happened at my place.

POLICEMAN It will happen here.

MAYOR No one left in the auditorium?

Third Man and Fourth Man peer down into the auditorium.

THIRD MAN No one.

MAYOR In the gallery?

FOURTH MAN Empty.

MAYOR Lock the doors. Don't let anyone into the auditorium.

The two men go into the auditorium.

THIRD MAN Locked.

FOURTH MAN Locked.

MAYOR   Turn off the lights. The full moon is shining through the gallery windows. That's enough.

The stage turns dark. In the dim moonlight, the people are only vaguely discernible.

MAYOR *(cont.)*   Form a lane.

The men of Güllen form a little lane. At its end stands the Gymnast, now dressed in elegant white trousers, a red sash across his muscle shirt.

MAYOR *(cont.)*   Pastor, if you please.

The Pastor slowly goes to Ill, sits down next to him.

PASTOR   Now, Ill, your time is at hand.

ILL   A cigarette.

PASTOR   A cigarette, Your Honor.

MAYOR *(warmly)*   Of course. A really good one.

He hands the pack to the Pastor, who offers it to Ill. Ill takes a cigarette, the Policeman gives him a light, and the Pastor hands the pack back to the Mayor.

PASTOR   As the prophet Amos said—

ILL   Please don't. *(Smokes.)*

PASTOR   You're not afraid?

ILL   Not much, any more. *(Smokes.)*

PASTOR *(helpless)*   I'll pray for you.

ILL   Pray for Güllen.

Ill smokes. The Pastor slowly rises.

PASTOR   God have mercy on us.

The Pastor slowly rejoins the Gülleners' ranks.

MAYOR   Rise, Alfred Ill.

Ill hesitates.

POLICEMAN   Get up, you son of a bitch. (*He drags Ill to his feet.*)

MAYOR   Officer, control yourself.

POLICEMAN   Excuse me. I lost it for a moment.

MAYOR   Come, Alfred Ill.

Ill drops the cigarette, extinguishes it with his foot. Then he slowly walks to the center of the stage, turning his back to the audience.

MAYOR (*cont.*)   Walk down the lane.

Ill hesitates.

POLICEMAN   Move.

Ill walks slowly into the lane of silent men. At its far end, the Gymnast stands facing him. Ill stops, turns around, sees the lane close mercilessly in on him, sinks to his knees. Without a sound, the lane turns into a cluster of bodies that swells and then slowly crouches down. Silence. Enter Newspaper Reporters downstage left. The lights go on.

JOURNALIST I   What's going on here?

The knot of bodies loosens, opens. The men gather silently upstage. Only the Doctor remains, kneeling in front of a corpse, which is covered with a checkered tablecloth of the kind used in restaurants. The Doctor stands up. Removes the stethoscope.

DOCTOR   Heart attack.

Silence.

MAYOR   Died of joy.

JOURNALIST I   Died of joy.

JOURNALIST II   Life writes the most beautiful stories.

JOURNALIST I   Let's get to work.

The Journalists hurry off upstage right. Claire Zachanassian enters left, followed by the Butler. She sees the corpse, stops, then slowly walks to the center of the stage, turning her back to the audience.

CLAIRE ZACHANASSIAN   Bring him here.

Roby and Toby come with a stretcher, put Ill on it, and place him before Claire Zachanassian's feet.

CLAIRE ZACHANASSIAN *(cont.)* *(motionless)*   Uncover him, Boby.

The Butler uncovers Ill's face. She looks at it for a long time, without moving.

CLAIRE ZACHANASSIAN *(cont.)*   Now he is again the way he was, a long time ago, the black panther. Cover him.

The Butler covers his face.

CLAIRE ZACHANASSIAN *(cont.)*   Carry him to the coffin.

Roby and Toby carry the body out, left.

CLAIRE ZACHANASSIAN *(cont.)*   Take me to my room, Boby. Get the bags packed. We're going to Capri.

The Butler offers her his arm, she walks slowly out toward the left, then stops.

CLAIRE ZACHANASSIAN *(cont.)*   Mayor.

The Mayor emerges from the row of silent men in the background and slowly comes forward.

CLAIRE ZACHANASSIAN (*cont.*)   The check. (*She hands him a piece of paper, then leaves with the Butler.*)

Just as improvements in the style and quality of clothing—discreet and inconspicuous, yet more and more apparent—expressed a rise in the standard of living, so the scenery has grown more and more appealing, changing imperceptibly as it, too, kept rising on the social ladder, much as if one were gradually moving from a slum into a modern, affluent neighborhood. Now, in the final tableau, this crescendo reaches its apotheosis. A previously gray world has been transformed into the flash and glitter of technical perfection, the epitome of affluence, a terminal happy end: flags, garlands, billboards, neon lights, women in evening gowns and men in tuxedos forming two choirs approximating those of Greek tragedy, not by coincidence but in an attempt at orientation, as if a foundering ship, swept far off course, were sending out its last signals.

CHORUS I

Many are the monstrous things of this world,
    Mighty earthquakes,
Tidal waves, fire-spewing mountains,
    And wars, too,
The clatter of tanks through cornfields,
    The mushroom cloud rivaling the sun.

CHORUS II

But none is more monstrous than poverty.
For poverty knows no adventure
    But only sows desolation,
Stringing day upon gloomy day
    Without end.

THE WOMEN

Helpless, the mothers watch
    Their loved ones wasting away.

THE MEN

But a man
Ponders rebellion
And meditates treason.

FIRST MAN

In worn-out shoes he walks the pavement

THIRD MAN

Foul-smelling weed between his lips

CHORUS I

For the jobs by which a man earned his bread
Are no longer

CHORUS II

And the great speeding trains shun his town.

ALL

Blessed are we

MRS. ILL

For a kindly fate

ALL

Has smiled upon us.

THE WOMEN

Appropriate clothing now graces
our delicate bodies

SON

The young man steers his sleek convertible

THE MEN

And the businessman his limousine

DAUGHTER

The young girl plays tennis on a brick-red court

DOCTOR
> Joyfully the surgeon wields the scalpel
>> In his new green-tiled operating room

ALL
> Our supper steams on the table.
> Content and well-shod
>> Everyone puffs a finer tobacco.

TEACHER
> Those who are avid for learning learn avidly

SECOND MAN
> The industrious executive heaps
>> Treasure upon treasure

ALL
> Rembrandt upon Rubens

PAINTER
> Art feeds the artist and is thus doubly fulfilling

PASTOR
> And filled to bursting with Christians
> On Christmas, Easter, and Whitsunday
>> Is the cathedral

ALL
> And the steam-spewing trains,
>> Majestic, gleaming,
> Flying fast on far-stretching tracks
>> From town to town, linking nations and peoples,
> Stop again at our station.

Enter Conductor, left.

CONDUCTOR Güllen.

STATIONMASTER Güllen-Rome Express, step in, please!
  Diner up front!

Claire Zachanassian emerges from upstage, motionless in her sedan chair, an old stone idol, advancing between the two choirs, accompanied by her entourage.

MAYOR
  The lady departs

ALL
  She who enriched us so greatly

DAUGHTER
  Our benefactress

ALL

With her noble entourage!

Claire Zachanassian exits, right. The last to leave are servants carrying the coffin in a long procession off the stage.

MAYOR
  May she fare well.

ALL
  Precious is the freight consigned
    To her safekeeping.

STATIONMASTER Stand clear!

ALL
  In these pounding, whirling times

PASTOR
  May a God

ALL

    Preserve us

MAYOR

    Our affluence

ALL

    Preserve our sacred goods, preserve
      The peace
    Preserve our freedom.
      Ward off the night
    Never to darken our town again,
      Our splendid, newly risen town,
    That we may enjoy our good fortune.